Please remember that this is a library book,
and that it belongs only temporarily to each
person who uses it. Be considerate. Do
not write in this, or any, library book.

WITHDRAWN

Critical Theory and Poststructuralism

IN SEARCH OF A CONTEXT

Mark Poster

Cornell University Press

ITHACA AND LONDON

First published 1989 by Cornell University Press.
First printing, Cornell Paperbacks, 1989.
Fifth printing 1996.

International Standard Book Number 0-8014-2336-8 (cloth)
International Standard Book Number 0-8014-9588-1 (paper)
Library of Congress Catalog Card Number 89-7262

Printed in the United States of America

*Librarians: Library of Congress cataloging information
appears on the last page of the book.*

♾ The paper in this book meets the minimum requirements of the American National Standard for Information Sciences—Permanence of Paper for Printed Library Materials, ANSI Z39.48-1984.

Contents

Acknowledgments

The Introduction and Chapters 3, 7, and 8 appear here for the first time. The other essays in this book have appeared elsewhere, although they have been revised, in some cases substantially, for this publication. Chapter 1 was published in Jack Trumpbour, ed., *International Perspectives on Europe*, vol. 1, *Politics and Society in Contemporary France and Germany* (Oxford and New York: Berg Publishers, 1989); Chapter 2 was published in *Notebooks in Cultural Analysis*, no. 1 (1984), 39–52; Chapter 4 appeared in *Cultural Critique*, 8 (Winter 1987–88), 105–22; Chapter 5 appeared in David Hoy, ed., *Foucault: A Critical Reader* (London: Blackwell, 1986), pp. 205–20. Chapter 6 appeared in Murray Krieger, ed., *The Aims of Representation: Subject/Text/History* (New York: Columbia University Press, 1987), pp. 107–30, copyright © 1987 by Columbia University, New York; used by permission.

During the years of writing these pieces my work was deeply influenced by discussions with my colleagues in the Critical Theory Institute at the University of California, Irvine. I am especially indebted to David Carroll, with whom I have enjoyed a continuing debate about theoretical concerns since the early 1970s. Chapter 6 was presented to the Critical Theory Institute and was enhanced by the institute's diversity of viewpoints and its lively, disputatious atmosphere of criticism and exchange of ideas. I have greatly benefited from discussions with Leslie Rabine, particularly concerning deconstruction and its relation to feminist theory. Allan Megill gave me detailed and thoughtful comments for improvement of the entire manuscript. His thorough, sympathetic criticism greatly assisted me in transforming what once were discrete essays into a coherent volume; his help is a model intellectual collegiality. Martin Jay carefully read the entire manuscript. His enormous erudition enhanced my writing in many places and his insightful knowledge of the Frankfurt School alerted me to many limitations of my discussion of that subject. My good friend Jonathan Wiener read parts of the manuscript and made helpful suggestions. John Rowe, also of the Critical Theory Institute, read Chapter 4 and Michael Clark read Chapter 6; both provided me with the benefit of their comments. The Critical Theory Institute and the Research and Travel fund of the School of Humanities at the University of California at Irvine generously supported my work on this book.

MARK POSTER

Irvine, California

Critical Theory and
Poststructuralism

Introduction: Theory and the Problem of Context

This book attempts a rapprochement between the tradition of critical social theory as developed by the Frankfurt School and other continental theorists, including Jean-Paul Sartre, and French poststructuralism, especially as practiced by Michel Foucault. The urgency of this confrontation, in my mind, is due to the inability of critical theory to sustain a convincing critique of the present social formation in face of the need for such a critique. Critical theory, as defined long ago by Max Horkheimer,[1] attempts to promote the project of emancipation by furthering what it understands as the theoretical effort of the critique of domination begun by the Enlightenment and continued by Karl Marx. I am in agreement with that restricted definition. Often, however, the term *critical theory* also implies the use of specific Marxist concepts, such as the dialectic, or includes an insistence on framing critical discourse in relation to some stage of capitalism.[2] I find this meaning of critical theory less useful because I think that in the present conjuncture the critique of capitalism serves to obscure the understanding of new forms of domination which have emerged during this century.

In the first half of the twentieth century Marxist theory suffered three setbacks: (1) the establishment of bureaucratic socialism in East-

[1]Max Horkheimer, "Traditional and Critical Theory," *Critical Theory: Selected Essays,* trans. Matthew O'Connell et al. (New York: Herder and Herder, 1972), pp. 188–243.
[2]Douglas Kellner, *Critical Theory, Marxism, and Modernity* (Baltimore: Johns Hopkins University Press, forthcoming).

ern Europe; (2) the rise of fascism in Central Europe; and (3) the birth of the "culture industry" in Western Europe and the United States. These massive phenomena reshuffled the dialectical deck of cards. No longer could it be said that the working class is the standard-bearer of freedom, the living negation of domination, the progressive side in contemporary class struggles that would surely end in a utopian community. The Frankfurt School reconstructed Marxism so as better to account for the new situation, especially for the ideological hegemony of capitalism and the cultural supremacy of mass society. But the Frankfurt School never adequately clarified its relation to Marxism.

The critique of the "culture industry" by Theodor Adorno, Max Horkheimer, and Herbert Marcuse waffled over the years between two positions. On the one hand, the critique of culture was theorized as a supplement to a Marxist understanding of capitalism. In Frankfurt School texts, workers, now considered "the masses," were viewed as manipulated, depoliticized, and reconciled to capitalist values by all aspects of popular culture. Jazz, astrology columns, sports, television, consumer goods generally—the entire panorama of leisure and daily life since World War II—narcotized and numbed the working class. The Frankfurt School presented a monochromatic picture of mass culture in which a dubious functionalist analysis operated. A unified and mystifying intention to disrupt the class struggle stood behind every manifestation of the culture industry. The discourse of the Frankfurt School staged contemporary life as a parody of crude capitalist greed and stupid working-class gullibility.

On the other hand, Adorno and Horkheimer, though perhaps not Marcuse, gave up on the working class. They began to despair over its negative, liberatory powers and therefore eased their resort to the capitalist mode of production as the foundation of their discourse. In their writings both the working-class subject and the bourgeois subject began to disappear from history. Adorno especially moved toward a "negative dialectic," a postulate of nonidentity and a remote appeal to critique as the last resort of a world without discernible hope for redemption. In both its theoretical modes—mass culture based on functionalist Marxism and Olympian critique based on negative dialectic—the critical power of Frankfurt School writings began to dissipate.

Today in the late twentieth century the situation has grown worse. This time critical theory has suffered three additional setbacks: (1) the decolonization movement has raised voices that question the ability of

Western thought to encompass the critique of Western forms of domination; (2) the feminist movement has uncovered patriarchal elements within Western theory, not excepting critical theory; (3) the social formation has been altered by electronic systems of communication, cybernetic devices, and a massive institutional growth of science, changes I lump together under the designation "mode of information." Albeit in very different ways, each of these developments calls into question not only the familiar social landscape that had been the target of critical theory but the subject of that theory—the position of the knower, the assumptions of the theorist that authorized him/her to write, that governed the shape of his/her discourse, that provided certain unexamined suppositions about the world, about writing, and about the relation of writing to the world.

Yet critical theory contains the best of what remains in the shambles of the Marxist and neo-Marxist theoretical positions, the best of what is left of the Left. It presents an attitude of antagonism and critique in the face of the deeply problematic contemporary social formation. It sustains an effort to theorize the present as a moment between the past and the future, thus holding up a historicizing mirror to society, one that compels a recognition of the transitory and fallible nature of society, one that insists that what is can be disassembled and improved considerably. Critical theory goes against the grain of a legitimating process endemic to power formations, a discursive mechanism through which the finitude of institutions is naturalized and universalized. Critical theory is a disruptive counterforce to the inscription on the face of social practices which says "Do not tamper with me for I am good, just, and eternal." Unlike some poststructuralist tendencies, critical theory springs from an assumption that we live amid a world of pain, that much can be done to alleviate that pain, and that theory has a crucial role to play in that process. It further assumes that any theorizing that occludes the sense of embeddedness in an imperfect world is complicit with that world. In all these ways, this volume steadfastly adheres to the position of critical theory.

My contention in this book is that poststructuralist theory has much to offer for the reconstruction of critical theory in the context of these late twentieth-century developments. Let me at this point characterize my use of the term *poststructuralist*. Poststructuralist writers, especially Michel Foucault, reevaluate the nature of the subject of theory and the theoretical subject, basing the reevaluation in large part on new ways of conceptualizing language. Poststructuralists question the easy assumption that the theoretical subject can generate a discourse that represents the real, unmasks domination in the real, without himself/herself introducing new forms of domination.[3] Poststructuralists criticize the assumption of much of modern thought that theoretical discourse is a direct expression of a truth in the theorist's mind, that this truth in some way captures historical reality, and that the question of freedom entails the appropriation of this truth by historical agents and their subsequent action to actualize it. Poststructuralists point to various ways in which language materially affects the relation of the theorist to his or her discourse and the ways in which the social field is composed of linguistic phenomena—Foucault's discourse/practice, Baudrillard's code, Derrida's *écriture*, Lyotard's phrases and *le différend*.

The term *poststructuralist*, local to certain intellectual circles in the United States, draws a line of affinity around several French theorists who are rarely so grouped in France and who in many cases would reject the designation. I am referring to thinkers such as Jacques Lacan, Michel Foucault, Jacques Derrida, Jean Baudrillard, Gilles Deleuze, and Jean-François Lyotard. The validity of the use of the term *poststructuralist* derives from certain vicissitudes of intercontinental intellectual history in the past two decades. These thinkers were influenced by and reacted against the formalism of structuralist linguistics and against the figure of the epistemological subject implied or explicitly defended by its theorists. They also at some earlier time in their lives adhered in one manner or another to Marxist theory, later entertained doubts about it, and subsequently developed an opposition to the French Communist party and to its use of theory. Yet substantial and serious differences obtain among the poststructuralists, differences I do not mean to minimize.[4]

---

[3]This is not to say that critical theorists were unaware of these problems. Theodor Adorno and perhaps Walter Benjamin, on the periphery of the Frankfurt School, certainly grappled with the impasses of the Cartesian subject. For Adorno, see especially *Negative Dialectics*, trans. E. B. Ashton (New York: Seabury, 1973), and *Aesthetic Theory*, trans. C. Lenhardt (New York: Routledge and Kegan Paul, 1984). For a useful introduction to Adorno, see Martin Jay, *Adorno* (London: Fontana, 1984).

[4]I discuss the intellectual history of poststructuralism in Chapter 1. It may be that the use of the term in the United States has something to do with the fact that the German and French theorists are unable to engage productively in discussions on serious issues. (Chapter 1 explores this problem.) Within the intellectual hothouse of Paris, where theoretical stars incite envy and ferociously compete with one another for air time, it is unlikely that a clear sense of common themes would emerge among the poststructuralists. At one point in the late seventies such leading figures as Foucault, Derrida,

In this book, I take the poststructuralist interpretive strategy, with its focus on language, and develop two themes: (1) that its critique of Western reason is largely correct and needs to be integrated into critical theory and (2) that its sense of the importance of language needs to be appreciated and theoretically deployed in the context of an emerging social world in which new forms of language are appearing and being disseminated; these language forms, in many cases electronically mediated, are increasingly shaping the culture and the subjects within that culture.[5] This book challenges critical theory to carry out an autocritique of its inscription of reason and moves a few steps in that direction. But it also challenges poststructuralist theory to contextualize its own position and begin the critique of the present, as Foucault urged near the end of his life.

The point of such an autocritique is not a global, antirationalist attack on "reason," as critics of poststructuralist positions often contend. The problem with Enlightenment, modernist, and Marxist deployments of "reason" concerns the association of reason with a configuration of the subject as autonomous and implicitly male, as a neutral, contextless "transcendental ego" capable of determining truth in a way that associates truth with ontological specifications. The critique of critical theory itself relies on discursive reason and cannot completely dissociate itself from such dependence. The aim of the critique I am recommending is to disrupt the configuration of associations that have in the modernist tradition been part and parcel of its deployment of reason. In particular I believe that a strategy of contextualizing theory serves to destabilize the concept of reason in its Enlightenment forms, to maintain a tension between discourse and situation, truth and fiction, theory and politics. My main concern in this book is to define the relation between theory and context and to outline a contemporary context (the mode of information) which post-

---

Baudrillard, Deleuze, and Lyotard seemed to be forming a common project. Then Baudrillard published *Oublier Foucault* at a critical point in the delicate negotiations, and my understanding is that the common project quickly evaporated. Because of deplorable Franco-German relations and inhospitable Parisian conditions, the United States has been, since the early 1970s, the major site of debates between traditions of critical theory and poststructuralism. The utility of the term *poststructuralist* must be decided not by French intellectuals, who are perhaps unduly affected by Parisian myopia, but by American theorists, whose situation is more propitious.

[5]Critical theory has not been totally uncognizant of language. In *The Theory of Communicative Action* (1981) Jürgen Habermas certainly moves in this direction. I discuss the adequacy of his effort in the body of this volume.

structuralist positions are admirably suited to investigate. One of the chief problems with earlier critical theory is that its definition of the context, capitalism, was inappropriate to and worked against the full elaboration of the most promising impulses of its analysis of mass culture.

I must also clarify my use of the term *theory* in this volume. Theory is routinely distinguished from empirical investigations. Theory explores the concepts and terms that are inevitably employed in studies of discrete phenomena. In this definition theory is a proper and necessary part of every field of study. But there is another sense of the term *theory* by which it is distinguished from philosophy. The term has been used in the United States to refer to a certain style of questioning the foundations of the disciplines in the humanities. Theory in this sense is decidedly inter- or transdisciplinary. This form of theory avails itself of recent continental writing as an aid in voicing dissatisfactions with the basic assumptions of the disciplines of philosophy, history, and literature. In a third recent usage of the term, in this case mostly in France, theory comes under a certain suspicion. As used by the French poststructuralists, theory often means unexamined, naive, or exaggerated claims about the truth value of one's discourse. The use of the term by the French Communist party is an example of what the poststructuralists have in mind. Theory is, for the poststructuralists, an epistemological attempt at conceptual clarification which spills over into a metaphysical gesture to regulate the terms of reality. The theoretical concept, they worry, places too much faith in the theorist's ability to make determinations, to fix identities, identities whose effect is political. The theorist is the arbiter who decides whose sense of what is going on will count as valid. The reader may have caught the irony in all this: certain American academics, myself included, calling themselves "theorists," turn to French positions they call "poststructuralist." The French thinkers refuse the title "theorist" as well as the designation "poststructuralist." Yet the writings of the French thinkers in question, particularly Derrida, have far greater currency in the United States than in France. In their sometimes hysterical criticism of French theory, traditionalist American academics forget that "poststructuralist theory" is a uniquely American practice. Americans have assimilated Foucault, Derrida, and the rest by turning their positions into "poststructuralist theory." Here is a remarkably complex example of what may happen in "the sea change," the movement of European ideas across the Atlantic.

In this book I use the term *theory* in the American sense, including its irony. In the American academic scene, theory serves as a useful counterforce to strong empiricist tendencies in the disciplines of literature, history, and the social sciences. In addition "theory" is important to the work of critical theory in that it provides a contextual framework in the following sense. The labor of theory or, better, one of its labors, I argue, is to relate conceptual advances to their context not to reduce them to it but, quite the opposite, to demonstrate that the link between discourse and society gives discourse its generalizing force while providing what Fredric Jameson has called a "cognitive mapping" of society. Precisely because discourse has some meaningful link to its context, it serves to illuminate that context and even to provide an understanding of the mechanisms of domination of that context. Just in this sense, I argue, one important feature of poststructuralist theory, thus far perhaps largely unexplored, rests with its ability to clarify a social order increasingly characterized by electronically mediated language constellations. In other words, the poststructuralist fascination with language occurs in an age when older language forms and uses are in crisis and new ones are being set in place. Theory for me, then, involves a nontotalizing totalization, a setting of poststructuralist positions in a world, and an understanding of that world as well as poststructuralist theory on the basis of those positions.

The problem of context or the situation is intractable and not profitably resolved by a hasty resort to a formula, such as Louis Althusser's determination in the last instance by the economy. Neo-Marxist strategies of framing the relation of one level of experience to another with such terms as *mediations* and *relative autonomy* indeed eliminate the most mechanical applications of that theory but are finally unsatisfying. In this study I treat the question of context not so much as the interplay of discrete social levels, as is characteristic of some social theory, or as a background to cultural works, as is typical in some literary history. For me, the question of context impinges on the work of the theorist in two ways. First, it forces the theorist to face the question of totalization or, in Foucault's term, "generality." To consider the context in which one is theorizing is a way to reflect upon the relative importance of the topic one is choosing to treat. It is to recognize that one is responsible as a person in a lifeworld for one's choice of subject matter. Second, by connecting one's theoretical domain to one's sociocultural world or to some aspect of it, one ensures in advance that one's discourse does not emanate from a transcendental ego, a subject sharply opposed to the realm of objects. In short the self-contextualized theorist acknowledges the will to power behind and within the truth claims of his/her discourse.

Historicism is the great exception to the advantages I claim for this way of contextualizing. Its leading exponent is Hegel, who takes as his context all of reality, infinitely expanding the scope of his situation and thereby reintroducing absolute truth claims. Marx begins more fruitfully in *The Communist Manifesto*, where he explicitly takes the point of view of the proletariat, recognizing that the truth of his discourse might legitimately be denied by those taking other perspectives, such as that of the bourgeoisie. Unfortunately Marx reintroduced difficulties when he then canonized the proletariat as a universal class, thereby delegitimating the perspectives of all other social groups. Even worse, this taking the point of view of a social subject (the proletariat) contains the danger of inferring that the position articulated by the theorist is identical with that of the social subject. A variation of the Freudian transference/countertransference is set in play between Marx and other Marxist theorists, on the one hand, and the proletariat, on the other. In this love affair the theorist may "stand in place of" rather than simply "take the point of view of" the social group. In its bad aspect, Marx's theory constitutes the working-class subject in the image of itself, introducing into capitalist society a supplementary form of domination specific to theory.

I find Nietzsche's treatment of the problem of context more fruitful. He set his discourse within the culture of his time, which he characterized as the age of the death of God and the demise of the slave morality. He invented a new kind of history, genealogy, to demonstrate the validity and value of that historical characterization. If we take it that his theory makes no claims for its truth value beyond what it may say about the contemporary context, we might be able to mitigate the ferocity of the charges that Nietzsche is a nihilist, a relativist, or irremediably stuck in a performative contradiction. We might also be able to avoid a degree of the transference/countertransference effect at play in the discourse of Marxism. The attraction of Nietzsche's position is that it attempts to theorize without constituting its readers as subjects, without introducing the theoretical domination effect that has played Western thought since Descartes, perhaps since Plato. But there are certainly no guarantees: the misuses of Marxism by Stalin are more than matched by the sad history of Nietzsche's appropriation by the Nazis.

Many American poststructuralists, especially deconstructionists, appear to believe that a political position and a social theory are built into their interpretive strategy. If one avoids closure and totalization in one's own discourse, they contend, if one unsettles, destabilizes, and complicates the discourses of the humanities, if one resists taking a stance of binary opposition in relation to the position one is criticizing, one has thereby instantiated a nonrepressive politics. Yet such a utopian epistemological vantage point may be more difficult to sustain than deconstructionists believe. Skeptics toward deconstruction are rightly bothered by the unique privilege it accords to language, by the unwillingness of deconstructionists to peek, even for an instant, outside an unending web of texts and signifiers. The vaunted careful or rigorous reading of the deconstructionist too easily becomes the excessively, obsessively cautious defense of his/her interpretation or reading. What I find most bothersome about deconstruction is that it is more wary of risking mistakes of theorizing and interpretation than of risking mistakes of social and political investigation. Deconstructionists fear the epithet "naive" more than they fear the charge of apoliticism.

While these caveats about deconstruction or even about poststructuralism generally may be partly justified, in some cases they are fueled by an assumption even more dangerous than the position they attack: the detractors of poststructuralism may be ignoring changes in the social world by which it has become constituted in part by simulacra, by copies with no originals, by an unending proliferation of images, by an infinitely regressive mirroring of word and thing, by a simultaneity of event and record of the event, by an instantaneity of act and observation, by an immediacy and copresence of electronically mediated symbolic interactions, by a language that generates its meanings to a large extent self-referentially. Time and space dimensions in our culture are undergoing vast, massive, and profound upheavals.

Linearity and causality are the spatial and temporal orderings of the now-bypassed modern era. Renaissance perspective and Newtonian physics encourage the individual to believe in the stability and continuity of the individual's position in a cultural/social world. From the standpoint of a subject thus constituted, language serves a representational function. The subject is the point of origin of meaning and the world consists in actions amenable to the understanding of that subject. We may christen that subject "Locke/Marx," envying perhaps the apparent stability of its culture, in which marks are securely locked in place.

Today language increasingly intervenes in a different configuration, which resists linear and causal framing. Words in our culture shamelessly point to themselves, like television newscasters who brashly admit their role in shaping the news, not simply reporting it. This self-referentiality of signs upsets the representational model of language, the assurance of reason to contain meaning, and the confidence in the ability of logical argument to determine the truth. The electronic mediation of communication in the postmodern lifeworld brings to the fore the rhetorical, figurative, performative, and self-reflexive features of language. These are precisely the aspects of language which poststructuralist hermeneutics is designed to delineate and make intelligible. In a world where Reagan's television persona gets him elected to the presidency, where the Soviets self-consciously rewrite their history, where commodities generate their demand and their use value through the signs they bear—in this postmodern world the line between words and things, subject and object, inside and outside, humanity and nature, idea and matter becomes blurred and indistinct, and a new configuration of the relation of action and language is set in place.

My purpose in this book is to reproblematize the critical social theory of this emerging postmodern world, to bring such theory to bear on poststructuralism, and to bring poststructuralism to bear upon it. In addition I attempt to rethink the parameters of critical theory once dialectical totalization and the autonomous subject of theory are no longer regarded as reliable foundations of the theoretical aspect of the project of emancipation. I regard this work as part of an ongoing, often painful effort of theoretical reorganization. I would like my work to be taken as tentative, as what one might call a heuristics, inviting others to improve on it if they are so inclined.

The essays in this book form a bridge between two of my recent projects: *Foucault, Marxism, and History* (1985) and *The Mode of Information* (unfinished). Chapter 1 is an assessment of the state of critical social theory today, focusing on the French poststructuralists and the German Frankfurt School. Chapters 2 and 3 go beyond the discussion of Western Marxism in *Foucault, Marxism, and History* by examining the notion of the self in Sartre and Foucault. Chapters 4 and 5 extend the investigation in the last chapter of *Foucault, Marxism, and History* by dealing with the questions of self-reflection and situation in Foucault in relation to works not discussed in the earlier book: Foucault's essay "What Is Enlightenment?" and his *History of Sexuality*, volumes 2 and 3, which had not appeared when I wrote the earlier book. Chapters 6, 7, and 8 form a bridge to my current project on the mode of information. Chapters 6 and 7 attempt to clarify this project beyond the cursory remarks at the end of *Foucault, Marxism, and History*. Chapter 8 focuses on the question of narcissism in contemporary culture and relates the theory of the mode of information to the family. It is based on a survey study I carried out in 1986.

1

The Modern versus
the Postmodern

In a recent overview of the current state of social theory, Perry Anderson laments, "Paris today is the capital of European intellectual reaction."[1] This judgment of 1984 refers not to the notoriously anti-Communist *nouveaux philosophes* but to the poststructuralists—Foucault, Derrida, Barthes, Lacan, Baudrillard, Lyotard, Deleuze—all of whom, Anderson notwithstanding, have participated in leftist politics and most of whom align themselves with the project of emancipation.[2] For Anderson the political climate in the mid-1980s is so conservative that he is able to name only one continental theorist of stature, Jürgen Habermas of Frankfurt-am-Main, who escapes the negative epithet. Indeed the current battle over theory, over the foundations of critical theory, may be studied as a duel between Habermas and the poststructuralists.

In some ways, the debate, however acrimonious, represents an improvement in Franco-German intellectual relations. Since the Enlightenment, French and German intellectuals have largely ignored one another despite geographical and at times even spiritual proximity. The exceptions to this situation, while important, are surprisingly few: Goethe's interest in Diderot, Marx's interest in Fourier and Saint-Simon, Victor Cousin's interest in Hegel, the symbolist poets' fascination with Wagner, Sartre's interest in Heidegger, the recent

[1]Perry Anderson, *In the Tracks of Historical Materialism* (Chicago: University of Chicago Press, 1984), p. 32.
[2]Barthes, Lacan, and Foucault are of course no longer alive.

interest of many French intellectuals in Nietzsche, and several other examples. Even if the list is doubled or tripled, the generalization would seem to hold that two proximate cultures have been well insulated from each other for two centuries. Americans are routinely astonished at the ignorance induced by the vapors of the Rhine. I recall asking Habermas in the mid-1970s if he had read Baudrillard, who also worked on the problem of language in critical social theory. "No, he had not," was the reply. Within the year I had the occasion to ask Baudrillard, who was trained as a Germanist, if he had read Habermas: no, he said, but he had heard of him. In this historical context the interest of the French poststructuralists in the Frankfurt School and the critical attention Habermas has given of late to the French, whatever their difficulties, must be taken as a step toward international understanding.

The current rift between Habermas and the French can be traced back to the politically intense days of 1968. While most French intellectuals supported the New Left, Habermas had serious difficulties with the German student movement, or at least with what he considered its excesses. His essay on the Socialistische Deutsche Studentenbund reproached them for their radical antiauthoritarianism, their regressive tendencies, and he advised the students to confine their reforming zeal to the halls of the university.[3] He warned that lack of working-class support for SDS limited its revolutionary potential. Discounting the fact that the eight or nine million French workers went on strike in solidarity with the students in that nation, Habermas surmised that these workers also "resisted" the May '68 events.[4] In the course of the late 1960s and early 1970s, Habermas at times softened his critique of the New Left.[5] French intellectuals were less grudging. The future poststructuralists hailed the Paris Spring as a new age in revolutionary struggle. Baudrillard, Foucault, Deleuze, Barthes, Derrida, Lyotard, Lacan—all discerned hopeful signs of democratization in the massive protest movement.[6]

[3]Jürgen Habermas, "The Movement in Germany," in *Toward a Rational Society*, trans. Jeremy Shapiro (Boston: Beacon, 1970), p. 46.

[4]Ibid., p. 37.

[5]See his comments in an interview published as "Political Experience and the Renewal of Marxist Theory," in Peter Dews, ed., *Habermas: Autonomy and Solidarity* (New York: Verso, 1987).

[6]For a critical view of the role of intellectuals in May 1968 from a conservative perspective, see Luc Ferry and Alain Renaut, *La pensée 68: Essai sur l'anti-humanisme contemporain* (Paris: Gallimard, 1985).

The disparity in the enthusiasms of Habermas and the French intellectuals for the politics of 1968 may be attributed in part to the difference in the nature of the movements in the respective nations. The radical students in Germany were isolated from wider political and social groups; the French were backed by popular opinion at large, by non-Communist unions, by Mitterrand and the Socialist party, by many skilled technical workers, and by virtually the entire artistic and intellectual community with the notable exceptions of Louis Althusser and Raymond Aron, united in an unusual moment of agreement. In response to this new political situation and to the general socioeconomic changes of "postindustrial society," Habermas and the French were moving in different directions. I will now summarize the two directions of thought to provide a background to the confrontation of their positions.

Recognizing general weaknesses in existing social theory, Habermas set out to "reconstruct" historical materialism.[7] He introduced the following revisions, rendered in broad, simplified outline:

(1) Define the conditions for a "public sphere," separate from private interests, which could serve as an arena for consensual reform.

(2) In advanced capitalism, the state enters the economy, shattering the superstructure/base distinction. The legitimacy of the state is in crisis because economic issues are now politicized.

(3) In advanced capitalism, science is integrated into the economy and takes its place as part of ideology.

(4) In the new social context, blind adherence to working-class politics must yield to a more general demand for the conditions of free public discussion. Marxist theory must be revised to account for what Habermas variously terms symbolic interaction, communicative action, or language.

(5) The problem of theory is to outline a universal pragmatics of language which may serve as the condition for public debate or, in his more controversial formulation, "the ideal speech situation."

(6) Since the problem is sociolinguistic, critical theory must ground

---

[7]Jürgen Habermas, *Zur Rekonstruktion des historischen Materialismus* (Frankfurt: Suhrkamp, 1976). For a good sense of the way Habermas's recent positions have been received in the English-speaking world, see John B. Thompson and David Held, eds., *Habermas: Critical Debates* (Cambridge: MIT Press, 1982); and for a reliable overview of Habermas's work, see Thomas McCarthy, *The Critical Theory of Jürgen Habermas* (Cambridge: MIT Press, 1978).

reason not in a concept of consciousness but in a concept of communicative action.

(7) The revised Habermasian dialectic now interprets history as a set of moral, cognitive, and aesthetic advances. In the current stage of history, autonomous rational individualism is possible if the conditions of communicative rationality are achieved. Such a moral change would align practical reason with the more developed instrumental reason, *wertrationalität* with *zweckrationalität*. This evolutionary schema is intended not as a classic philosophy of history but as a heuristic model that can orient concrete studies.[8]

The French poststructuralists look at things very differently.[9] They are particularly concerned with the foundation and limits of theory. They are animated by a rereading of Nietzsche, especially by his far-reaching and virulent critique of truth.[10] The lesson they learn from Nietzsche is that truth is not a transcendent unity. The persistent attempt in European philosophy to unify truth, be it by means of a scientific method or through a dialectical totalization, has unfortunate epistemological and political implications. The tendency in poststructuralism is therefore to regard truth as a multiplicity, to exult in the play of diverse meanings, in the continual process of reinterpretation, in the contention of opposing claims. Accordingly, text replaces mind as the locus of enunciation, and difference replaces identity as the strategy of reading. Those not sensitive to what the poststructuralists regard as the epistemological dangers of consensual truth are highly

[8]Jürgen Habermas, *Strukturwandel del Öffenlichkeit* (Neuwied: Luchterhand, 1971); Habermas, *Legitimation Crisis*, trans. Thomas McCarthy (Boston: Beacon, 1975); Habermas, "Technology and Science as 'Ideology,'" in *Toward a Rational Society*, pp. 81–122; Habermas, *Communication and the Evolution of Society*, trans. Thomas McCarthy (Boston: Beacon, 1979); Habermas, *The Theory of Communicative Action*, vol. 1: *Reason and the Rationalization of Society*, trans. Thomas McCarthy (Boston: Beacon, 1984); Habermas, "History and Evolution," *Telos* 39 (Spring 1979), 5–44.

[9]For an opposing view of the relative merits of Habermas and the French poststructuralists, see Peter Dews, *Logics of Disintegration: Post-structuralist Thought and the Claims of Critical Theory* (New York: Verso, 1987). For an interesting viewpoint on the debate from what appears to be a Leo Straussian position, see Stanley Rosen, *Hermeneutics as Politics* (New York: Oxford University Press, 1987). If Dews, a Marxist, and Habermas, a critical theorist, see the poststructuralists as deviating from the modernist tradition in the direction of irrationalism, Rosen sees no significant break between the modern and the postmodern, between Kant and Derrida.

[10]The important but by no means the only essay in the rereading of Nietzsche is Gilles Deleuze, *Nietzsche and Philosophy*, trans. Hugh Tomlinson (New York: Columbia University Press, 1983; orig. edition 1962).

irritated by this celebration of "the undecidable," to mention one of Derrida's terms.

Having abandoned the assumption of the transcendent unity of truth, of truth as a totalizing closure, poststructuralists redefine the position of the theoretical subject and its relation to politics. The place of theory cannot be a center, a privileged locus, a solid point of origin for the progressive movement of society, either in a liberal or a Marxist sense. When theory is the ground of politics, the results are invariably authoritarian as the Jacobin and Leninist examples indicate. Favoring a strategy of the dispersal of truth, poststructuralists also take a cue from Nietzsche's association of truth with power. Truth is enunciated in discourses. These in turn are coordinated with power or, better, are forms of power since they shape practices. Far from the Olympian position of the *cogito*, they perceive truth as, at one level, a mundane, "always already" political affair, a multiplicity of claims without a final arbiter.

The theorist's situation, for poststructuralists, contains certain dangers. Theorizing with no guarantee of certain truth, poststructuralists seem to many observers to be in a cynical or, as Habermas argues, conservative position. These critics see little difference between the poststructuralist retreat from theory and similar moves by figures as diverse as Edmund Burke and Karl Popper. The response of Foucault, Derrida, and Lyotard, however, is that the quest for certain truth and the claim of having attained it are the greater dangers. The logocentric philosophical tradition, with its strong assertions about truth, is complicit, for them, in the disasters and abominations of twentieth-century Western history. On this difficult, even tragic issue of the relation of politics to truth, poststructuralists in general strive for a cosmopolitan position that makes every effort to recognize differences, even uncomfortable or disagreeable ones, and for a theory of truth that is wary of patriarchal and ethnocentric tendencies that hide behind a defense of reason as certain, closed, totalized. Above all, poststructuralists want to avoid forms of political oppression that are legitimized by resorts to reason, as this kind of legitimation has been, in their view, one of the paradoxical and lamentable developments of recent history. In the end it seems to me that the poststructuralists have by no means attained their goal of developing a nonauthoritarian form of discourse, and they are even farther from achieving an adequate politics consonant with that discourse.[11]

[11]The current state of poststructuralist thought on politics can be evaluated by looking at the recent spate of books on Heidegger, the Nazis, and the Jews. This discussion is

With these necessarily simplified characterizations of the positions before us, I can now turn to the confrontation of Habermas and the poststructuralists. The poststructuralists hold no uniform view of the Frankfurt School. Lacan and Barthes rarely, if ever, refer to it directly, though Barthes's *Mythologies* has affinities with Adorno's analysis of the media. Deleuze's *Anti-Oedipus* explicitly opposes the Freudian-Marxist synthesis associated with the Frankfurt School in the works of the early Fromm, Horkheimer's *Studien über die Familie*, and Marcuse's *Eros and Civilization*.[12] Nonetheless his call to liberate the schizoid impulses of the libido might be viewed as a variation on the Freudian-Marxist theme. As for Derrida, I recall seeing but a single mention of the Frankfurt School or its members in any of his works.[13] Baudrillard's case is more complex. His early works directly parallel the themes of the Frankfurt School, though after 1972 his position drifts more and more away from that problematic.[14] Lyotard's writings have been the most explicitly antagonistic to the Germans. The collection of essays *Des dispositifs pulsionnels* mounts a strong attack against the Frankfurt School, especially Adorno's negative dialectic. *The Postmodern Condition* is equally vehement against Habermas.[15]

Foucault is the only poststructuralist who actively sought to associate his work with that of the Frankfurt School. In *Discipline and Punish*, Foucault criticizes an obscure neo-Marxist analysis of prisons by two associates of the Frankfurt School, George Rusche and Otto Kirchheimer. At the time, in 1975, even this attention to work by the

highly complex, but one of its motifs is the relation of philosophy to politics. See Philippe Lacoue-Labarthe, *La fiction du politique* (Paris: Bourgois, 1987); Victor Farias, *Heidegger et le nazisme*, trans. Myriam Benarroch and Jean-Baptiste Grasset (Paris: Verdier, 1987); Jacques Derrida, *De l'esprit: Heidegger et la question* (Paris: Galilée, 1987); Jean-François Lyotard, *Heidegger et "les juifs"* (Paris: Galilée, 1988); Avital Ronel, *The Emergency Call: A Politics of Technology* (Lincoln: University of Nebraska Press, 1988).

[12]Fromm's early essays are collected in Erich Fromm, *The Crisis of Psychoanalysis: Essays on Freud, Marx, and Social Psychology* (New York: Fawcett, 1970).

[13]The only exception is Walter Benjamin in Derrida's *The Truth in Painting*, trans. Geoff Bennington and Ian McLeod (Chicago: University of Chicago Press, 1987), but he was on the periphery of the Frankfurt School.

[14]Baudrillard's early works would include *Le système des objets* (1968), *La société de consommation* (1970), and *Pour une critique de l'économie politique du signe* (1972). For a selected overview of his writings, see Mark Poster, ed., *Baudrillard: Selected Writings*, trans. Jacques Mourrain (Stanford: Stanford University Press, 1988).

[15]See Jean-François Lyotard, "Adorno come diavolo," in *Des dispositifs pulsionnels* (Paris: 10/18, 1973), pp. 115–33, trans. by Robert Hurley as "Adorno as the Devil," in *Telos* 19 (Spring 1974), 127–37; Jean-François Lyotard, *The Postmodern Condition: A Report on Knowledge*, trans. Geoff Bennington and Brian Massumi (Minneapolis: University of Minnesota Press, 1984).

Frankfurt School was exceptional in France. Foucault refers to Rusche and Kirchheimer's "great work" as providing "a number of essential reference points" for his own analysis.[16] Though Foucault's analysis differs considerably from that of the Frankfurt School, he respected it enough to pay these compliments. On a number of occasions Foucault complained that his own education in France offered no introduction to the work of the Germans: "When I was a student I can assure you that I never heard the name of the Frankfurt School mentioned by any of my professors."[17] The project that increasingly engaged Foucault's interest toward the end of his life was a critique of scientific reason, which the Frankfurt School, following Weber, had pioneered and explored at length. While Foucault was not completely happy with the direction of the Germans' work, he was eager to cooperate with Habermas and others in what he saw as a common enterprise.

If the poststructuralists' attitude toward the Frankfurt School was mixed, the same cannot be said of Habermas's disposition to the French. From the Adorno Prize address of 1980 to the Boston speech of 1982 to the Paris lectures of 1984, Habermas took the occasions of public-speaking engagements to denounce the dangerous errors of the French poststructuralists.[18] Before that time, Habermas paid scant notice to philosophy across the Rhine. Martin Jay, the noted historian of the Frankfurt School, rightly observes that Habermas is no sectarian who restricts his interests to a narrow circle of thinkers. Habermas, Jay points out, bolsters his position with "arguments of a wide range of thinkers, most notably Weber, Luhmann, Parsons, Piaget and Kohlberg."[19] Indeed Habermas is truly a cosmopolitan intellectual, taking

[16]Michel Foucault, *Discipline and Punish: The Birth of the Prison*, trans. Alan Sheridan (New York: Pantheon, 1977), pp. 24–32. It is of course difficult to know how seriously to take Foucault's praise in this sentence.

[17]Gérard Raulet, "Structuralism and Post-structuralism: An Interview with Michel Foucault," trans. Jeremy Harding, *Telos* 55 (Spring 1983), 200, and also in conversations I had with him.

[18]These are, respectively, Habermas, "Modernity versus Postmodernity," *New German Critique* 22 (Winter 1981), 3–18; Habermas, "The Entwinement of Myth and Enlightenment," *New German Critique* 26 (Spring/Summer 1982), 13–30; and Habermas, *Der philosophische Diskurs der Moderne: Zwöfe Vorlesungen* (Frankfurt: Suhrkamp, 1984), published in English as *The Philosophical Discourse of Modernity*, trans. Frederick Lawrence (Boston: MIT Press, 1987). Habermas first mentions Foucault in a 1977 essay, "Ideologies and Society in the Post-war World," referring to him as an anarchist, as is noted in Jürgen Habermas, *Autonomy and Solidarity: Interviews*, ed. Peter Dews (London: Verso, 1986), p. 46. In a 1978 essay whose title might be translated as "Conservatism and capitalist crisis," which appeared in Italian, Foucault fell into "irrationalism."

[19]Martin Jay, "Habermas and Modernism," *Praxis International* 4 (April 1984), 5,

cues where he finds them, except, that is, from France. Jay's list of influences on Habermas includes, after all, two Germans, two Americans, and a Swiss.[20] In the 1980s, then, Habermas's relation to French poststructuralism shifted from simple avoidance to an outburst of hostility. In estimating the reasons for the change one would want to take into account that during the early 1980s Habermas had just completed his major work of reconstructing Marxism as a defense of Enlightenment rationality. *The Theory of Communicative Action* appeared in 1981 in two large volumes. Perhaps the time was ripe to turn one's attention to opposing points of view, and what better place to search for those than across the Rhine?

Habermas casts his differences with the poststructuralists as a debate over the nature of modernity. He defines modernity in the sociological terms of Max Weber as the process of the differentiation of science, morality, and art into autonomous spheres. Modernization is the fulfillment of each of these spheres and their incorporation into the lifeworld, the full development of each sphere and the subsequent transformation of daily life on the basis of that perfection. What was missing from Weber's definition, in Habermas's eyes, was a specification of the conditions in everyday life which enabled the transfer of science, morality, and art back onto society. In *The Theory of Communicative Action*, Habermas provided those conditions with the concept of the universal pragmatics of language. If public speech were structured properly the autonomous cultural domains of science, morality, and art would be integrated into society, thereby achieving human emancipation, that is, the synthesis of reason and society and the fulfillment the project of modernity as outlined by the Enlightenment.

According to Habermas the French move to postmodernity was a retreat from the challenge of the Enlightenment, not an advance beyond it. What bothered Habermas most about the French rejection of the Enlightenment project was its critique of reason and resort to counterrationalist positions like those of Georges Bataille and Martin

---

reprinted in Richard Bernstein, ed., *Habermas and Modernity* (Oxford: Blackwell, 1985), pp. 125–39. In an interview with Perry Anderson, Habermas listed some fifteen of those who had influenced him. Nearly all were German, and only Emile Durkheim was French. See "Jürgen Habermas: A Philosophico-Political Profile," *New Left Review* 151 (May–June 1985), 76.

[20]It might also be noted that the French were absent from the well-known collection of debates with Habermas, *Habermas: Critical Debates*, ed. John B. Thompson and David Held (Cambridge: MIT Press, 1982), which included a reply by Habermas. The critics were British, American, and West German in approximately equal numbers.

Heidegger. In 1981, then, the French, in a "line" that led "from Bataille via Foucault to Derrida," were "Young Conservatives" who had turned their backs on the unfinished the project of modernity. In 1982 the poststructuralists, disciples of Nietzsche's antirationalism, betrayed a "regressive turn [that] enlists the powers of emancipation in the service of counter-enlightenment."[21] By 1984 Habermas had undertaken an intensive investigation of the French writers. His lectures of that year demonstrate a sustained, systematic reading of poststructuralist authors. Habermas's masterful ability to digest vast corpuses of theory and to analyze them rigorously in relation to his own position is brilliantly on display once more in the Paris lectures.[22] But the intensive reading of the French texts did not alter Habermas convictions. In 1985 he complained that poststructuralism "bails out" on the Enlightenment, falsely thinking it can find a "cure for the wounds of Enlightenment other than the radicalized Enlightenment itself."[23] Finally, in 1986 he said that the French "mystify peculiarly modern experiences."[24]

A full treatment of Habermas's position on poststructuralism would require a detailed evaluation of *The Philosophical Discourse of Modernity*, which is largely based on lectures given in Paris and Ithaca, New York. While there is no space for such a discussion in the context of this essay, one peculiarity of the book is worth pointing out: Habermas appropriates the poststructuralist critique of reason for his own ends. Instead of condemning the French attack on Enlightenment humanism, Habermas surprisingly argues that he does it better than they do. He attributes to his own theory of communicative action, not to deconstruction and not to discourse analysis, the true critique of logocentric reason:

---

[21]Habermas, "Modernity versus Postmodernity," p. 13; Habermas, "Entwinement of Myth and Enlightenment," p. 29.

[22]Habermas, *Der philosophische Diskurs der Moderne*.

[23]Anderson, "Jürgen Habermas," p. 82.

[24]Jürgen Habermas, *Autonomy and Solidarity: Interviews*, ed. Peter Dews (London: Verso, 1986), 203. The full quotation reads: "[The French thinkers project the experience of unreason] backwards into archaic origins, onto the Dionysian, the pre-Socratic, the exotic and primitive. This kind of *nachgeahmte Substantialität* was completely alien to Adorno and Benjamin. It never occurred to them to mystify peculiarly modern experiences in this fashion. For that is what this radical criticism of reason in effect amounts to, with its fabulation of precivilizational states. We have had all that, in Germany, so immediately at hand that you can smell it ever afterwards: the artificial mystification of something so close into something supposedly so primordial." Poststructuralism is thus equated with the underlying mythologies of the Third Reich.

The furious labor of deconstruction has identifiable consequences only when the paradigm of self-consciousness, of the relation-to-self of a subject knowing and acting in isolation, is replaced by a different one—by the paradigm of mutual understanding, that is, of the intersubjective relationship between individuals who are socialized through communication and reciprocally recognize one another. Only then does the critique of the domineering thought of subject-centered reason emerge in a *determinate* form —namely, as a critique of Western "logocentrism," which is diagnosed not as an excess but as a deficit of rationality.[25]

The important shift in Habermas's argument in this passage, and therefore in the impact of the book as a whole, is that Habermas ascribes to his own position the critique of Enlightenment reason which is at the heart of the poststructuralist position. Poststructuralism serves Habermas well by filling a gap in his own argument. His *Theory of Communicative Action* introduced a shift from a problematic of consciousness to one of language, but the justification for this move was not adequately explained. A major weakness in Habermas's position, one that dates back to his essays from the late 1960s, is the flat-footedness in his move from the concept of labor to concepts of "symbolic interaction," "language," or "mutual understanding." This move (away from classical Marxism) is presented as a simple supplement or addition to an existing position. Until *The Philosophical Discourse of Modernity* Habermas never persuasively argued this shift or cogently justified it. Poststructuralism provided Habermas with a sharp critique of the inadequacy of Marx's position on reason, the legacy of this flaw in his concept of labor, and the resulting need to rethink critical theory from a perspective rooted in language theory. In a sense, therefore, Habermas's conquest of Rome from the north has made him something of a Roman. But his self-presentation as the one who has done properly what the French do badly undermines his critique of poststructuralism as "irrationalism" and calls his own project into question. For himself, Habermas claims that he has merely given up a false concept of reason in favor of a more suitable one.

Habermas's attack on poststructuralism is most revealing when he is compelled to distinguish the positions of Horkheimer and Adorno in *Dialectic of Enlightenment* from those of the French. The Frankfurt School itself, it could be argued, preceded poststructuralists in the critique of the Enlightenment. In the dark days of the 1940s the forces

---

[25]Habermas, *Philosophical Discourse of Modernity*, p. 310.

of science and reason appeared to promote, not to dissipate, domination. There are no more fitting testimonies to the Nietzschean critique of reason than the technical rationality in the organization of Auschwitz and the scientific creativity of the Manhattan Project, which made Hiroshima feasible. Adorno and Horkheimer did not shrink from the fact that enlightenment produced economical mass extermination in gas chambers and instant incineration with the atom bomb. No wonder Foucault admired the work of the Frankfurt School: the Germans, like the Frenchman, were impressed with the interconnection of reason and power, reason as technical mastery becoming the domination and destruction of human beings. The Baconian maxim "knowledge is power" received new meaning in the 1940s.

Faced with the disturbing pessimism of *Dialectic of Enlightenment*, Habermas pleads for a judicious, balanced judgment and declares that "bourgeois ideals" contain "elements of reason." Habermas writes:

I mean the internal theoretical dynamic which constantly propels the sciences—and the self-reflection of the sciences as well—*beyond* the creation of merely technologically exploitable knowledge; furthermore, I mean the universalist foundations of law and morality which have *also* been embodied (in no matter how distorted and imperfect a form) in the institutions of constitutional states, in the forms of democratic decision-making, and in individualistic patterns of identity formation; finally, I mean the productivity and the liberating force of an aesthetic experience with a subjectivity set free from the imperatives of purposive activity and from the conventions of everyday perception.[26]

But Horkheimer and Adorno and the poststructuralists do not dispute that there are "elements of reason" in liberal culture. What they dispute is the lens that discerns "reason" in law and democracy but not in gas chambers and atom bombs, the distorted Habermasian lens that espies in bourgeois reason a mirage of "universalist foundations" when there is nothing more in sight than yet another human discourse. When Habermas defends with the label of reason what he admires in Western culture, he universalizes the particular, grounds the conditional, absolutizes the finite.[27] He provides a center and an

[26]Habermas, "Entwinement of Myth and Enlightenment," p. 18.

[27]There may well be a political motive for Habermas's defense of bourgeois liberties, since the Federal Republic of Germany has recently suffered a wave of repression similar to that of the McCarthy era in the United States. Fredric Jameson discusses this situation in "The Politics of Theory: Ideological Positions in the Postmodernism Debate," *New German Critique* 33 (Fall 1984), 59. Whatever may be the humane benefits of such a political intervention, they still do not justify, at the level of theory, an absolutist defense of reason.

origin for a set of discursive practices. He undermines critique in the name of critique by privileging a locus of theory (reason) that far too closely resembles society's official discourse.

Of course two different things are being spoken about and confounded, as is the case in many disputes. Like Weber, Habermas distinguishes between instrumental rationality and communicative rationality. Instrumental rationality characterizes practices in what he calls "the system," that is in institutions like the bureaucratic state and the economy, which achieve social solidarity through "steering mechanisms." Communicative rationality characterizes actions in what he calls the lifeworld, that is, in areas of social action where socialization and cultural reproduction are at issue. Communicative rationality designates the ability of speakers to raise "validity claims" to those they address and to problematize those claims in a general effort to achieve mutual understanding. When the "system" intrudes upon the "lifeworld," as it increasingly does in technically advanced societies, "pathologies" are produced. Communicative action is aborted because efforts at mutual understanding are replaced by hierarchically distorted verbal exchanges in which each party instrumentally manipulates the other, with the state, for example, having a considerable advantage in the manipulation game over a welfare mother.[28]

Communicative rationality, in Habermas's view, is not subject to the poststructuralist critique of reason. Only instrumental reason supports domination and is therefore open to the poststructuralist objection. Communicative rationality requires a democratic context in which anyone may question the argumentative claims of anyone else, so long as each party aims at consensus and agrees to concur with positions that he or she cannot refute. The issue in the Franco-German debate is whether such a notion of consensus contains elements of domination. Lyotard, for one, thinks that it does, that the "sort of unity Habermas has in mind" is restrictive in the postmodern context, which is characterized precisely by a multiplicity of cultural expressions (le différend).[29] Habermas's notion of reason as consensus, in Lyotard's view, introduces constraints upon the most desirable manifestations of cultural development in postmodernity: the play of unrecuperable differences. No sharper opposition can be posed than this:

[28]Jürgen Habermas, *The Theory of Communicative Action*, vol. 2: *Lifeworld and System: A Critique of Functionalist Reason*, trans. Thomas McCarthy (Boston: Beacon, 1987), p. 183.
[29]Jean-François Lyotard, "Answering the Question: What Is Postmodernism?" trans. Régis Durand in *The Postmodern Condition* (Minneapolis: University of Minnesota, 1984), p. 72.

Habermas defending reason in the form of consensus and Lyotard denouncing reason as a danger to dissensus. From a certain vantage point, Habermas and Lyotard appear to veer toward one another, despite their acrimonious hostility. Habermas wants to allow for critique and dissent as determinants of public policy; Lyotard implies but does not assert a consensus over differences, that his reader ought to assent to the justice of his claim for the play of multiple of discourses. Yet beneath this point of convergence a fundamental opposition divides the two positions: Habermas defends modernity as the *rationality* of communicative action; Lyotard defends the postmodernity of an *aesthetic* model of a multiplicity of cultures. One may enunciate the issue at stake as follows: which of these positions better accounts for critique in the context of postindustrial society, or what I call the mode of information? To the extent that Habermas's position can be said to presuppose or support a notion of the subject which invokes the autonomous individual of bourgeois society and the class consciousness of the proletariat, his position recuperates the elements of domination in the "dialectic of enlightenment." To the extent that Lyotard opens the scene for the entry of hitherto excluded configurations of subjectivity (women, gays, minorities), his position must be said to compose a critical posture against established forms of authority. If no form of freedom is possible beyond that envisaged in the metanarratives of liberalism and Marxism, however, Habermas secures more firmly than Lyotard existing levels of democracy, and Lyotard, by challenging that democracy, opens the path to directions that may regress beneath whatever freedom is currently enjoyed.

In my view, Habermas seriously underestimates the difficulties of the current conjuncture in democratic societies. His defense of reason appropriates highly dangerous discursive practices. He uncritically legitimizes science, for example, as an achievement of consensus: "Modern science . . . [is] governed by ideals of an objectivity and impartiality secured through unrestricted discussion."[30] Yet modern science largely operates with an exclusion of women and minorities from its discourse, an exclusion that is legitimated precisely by the apparent procedural neutrality of "unrestricted discussion," of communicative rationality. Modern science instantiates the figure of the rational individual; it constitutes the subject of its discourse in a thor-

---

[30]Habermas, *The Theory of Communicative Action*, 2:91.

oughly Cartesian manner that discounts the value of rhetoric, fiction, and art and invalidates the voices of culturally determined subjects, such as women, who somehow do not have the "communicative competence" to engage in "unrestricted discussion."

Habermas claims simultaneously (1) that this notion of reason is counterfactual, that it has never existed and will never exist, and (2) that all of human history is moving toward a condition in which this communicative reason may become actual. He thus eats from the table of communicative reason as a universal necessity of logic and yet keeps it for another day as a historical tendency that is being actualized in the successive release of communicative competence in the modern world. He argues that this double strategy, simultaneously transcendental and empirical, avoids the element of domination characteristic of the same posture in earlier formulations of Enlightenment reason. In different ways Adorno, Horkheimer, Foucault, and Derrida agree that the dilemma of reason is that it postulates itself as transcendent, thereby constituting the world as one of objects, while it also empirically positions reason as another thing in the world. This subject/object identity, or "birth of man," introduces domination into those discourses, such as science, which ground themselves in transcendental reason while figuring empirical subjects as also rational. When Habermas reinscribes reason in the new register of communicative action he reproduces this doubling effect as the rhetorical figure of his own discourse. He writes, for example, "Society's knowledge of itself is concentrated neither in philosophy nor in social theory."[31] "Society's knowledge of itself" is contained in Habermas's discourse as the imperative to act so as to bring about consensus, to release potentials of communicative competence, to utter speech with the aim of mutual understanding. His own discourse contains the same hidden "performative contradiction" he attributes to his French opponents: to read the *Theory of Communicative Action* as an instance of communicative reason, fictionally to establish communicative rationality as the already existing empirical context of its very enunciation and emergence as a position, to accord to Habermas the privilege of an authorial voice with no illocutionary or rhetorical aims so that his position, his defense of communicative reason may emerge without the violence or force that represses oppositions to itself.

According to Habermas, Horkheimer and Adorno manage to pre-

---

[31]Habermas, *Philosophical Discourse of Modernity*, p.377.

serve the critical function, whereas Nietzsche and the poststructuralists undermine it. An inverse hypothesis works much better: *Dialectic of Enlightenment* is a product of disenchantment and despair with the universalizing values of reason, be they liberal or Marxist. Poststructuralists move a step beyond this negative reversal: the problem for the poststructuralists is not that reason has "turned into" domination but that all discourses are always already implicated in power. The problem is not that an absolute ground has been swept out from under us by certain historical events but that such grounds are the source of the theoretical problem in the first place. Adorno and Horkheimer historicize their critique of Enlightenment reason; the poststructuralists also treat it at the levels of epistemology and language.[32]

Confronting this dilemma, the American philosopher Richard Rorty provides an interesting alternative point of view. He rejects the solutions of both Habermas and the poststructuralists, opting instead for the pragmatism of John Dewey and disposing of the baby of critique along with the bath water of universal reason. Rorty writes, "What links Habermas to the French thinkers he criticizes is the conviction that the story of modern philosophy . . . is an important part of the story of the democratic societies' attempts at self-reassurance."[33] With a pose of humility not atypical of an Anglo-American philosopher, he suggests that social emancipation has nothing to do with theoretical critique. If Habermas wants emancipation, Rorty argues, he should work on concrete reforms; if the French want elegant theory they should practice it for its own sake. The disarming simplicity of Rorty's position is a tribute to the American discipline of philosophy. In short, why all the fuss, why bother with critique? As a literary critic remarked in a similar spirit, responding to a talk in which Edward Said pleaded for politically engaged criticism, in effect, "We don't need it. We are comfortable enough as we are."[34]

[32]Again *The Philosophical Discourse of Modernity* introduces subtle confusions. Habermas slides from an effort to keep the Frankfurt School separate from the French poststructuralists and ends by lumping the two into the same camp. In the conclusion of the book Habermas *fully includes* Adorno in the camp of the poststructuralists: "The radical critique[s] of reason . . . give no account of their own position. Negative dialectics, genealogy, and deconstruction alike avoid those categories in accord with which modern knowledge has been differentiated" (p. 336). Thus Adorno's negative dialectics is *no different from* Foucault's genealogy or Derrida's deconstruction.

[33]Richard Rorty, "Habermas and Lyotard on Postmodernity," *Praxis International* 4 (April 1984), 38.

[34]Oral intervention at a conference at State University of New York, Binghamton, in 1978. Edward Said's paper is available as "Reflections on Recent American 'Left' Literary

The pragmatist position paradoxically assumes the same Cartesian position it rejects. Descartes, Rorty complains, gave us "the false lead . . . that made us think truth and power *were* separable."[35] The defense of the *cogito* is thus, for him, the exemplar of all the difficulties. But if truth and power are not separable, as he argues in agreement with the poststructuralists, then how can one struggle for democratic reform without reference to discursive truth? The answer is not that theoretical discourse is extra baggage on the voyage to a free society but that it cannot be avoided. And if it cannot be avoided, the issue becomes, as both Habermas and the poststructuralists recognize, how may the discourse of theory intervene in practice without bolstering domination? The sorry truth for the American philosopher is that the difficult labor of sublimation is not a language game played only in the fields of academe but one inextricably entangled in the fate of society.

Habermas insists that theory must find a universal ground in reason. He claims to have done so in the historically totalized concept of the ideal speech situation, the universal pragmatics of language which provides validity claims for public discourse in nations that have attained moral maturity. The poststructuralists disagree with this conclusion but seriously differ among themselves about the best discursive strategy to choose. Baudrillard offers to decode the new age of "hyperreality" in which self-referential media languages constitute simulacra of communications. Derrida proposes an interminable deconstruction of the Western philosophical tradition, interminable because the internal structure of writing is trapped in an abyss of binary oppositions. Lyotard advocates a celebration of multiple, competing discourses, an acceptance of the justice of the *différend*, of the impossibility of consensus. Foucault proposes the self-constitution of the critical theorist through a practice of opposition to the dominant discourses of the present conjuncture.[36] While none of these provisional

Criticism," in William Spanos et al., eds., *The Question of Textuality: Strategies of Reading in Contemporary American Criticism* (Bloomington: Indiana University Press, 1982), pp. 11–30.

[35]Rorty, "Habermas and Lyotard on Postmodernity," p. 42.

[36]Baudrillard's most recent statement of this position can be found in *Les stratégies fatales* (Paris: Grasset, 1983). To my thinking the best statement of Derrida's position remains *Writing and Difference*, trans. Alan Bass (Chicago: University of Chicago Press, 1978). For Lyotard's view, see Jean-François Lyotard, *Le différend* (Paris: Minuit, 1983). Foucault's position was being elaborated in the multivolume project *The History of Sexuality* when his life abruptly ended. See, for example, Michel Foucault, *The Use of Pleasure*, trans. Robert Hurley (New York: Pantheon, 1985).

interpretive stances is entirely adequate (nor are they claimed to be so), none of them is fairly labeled "conservative" or "counterrevolutionary." In my view, each has the advantage over Habermas in squarely facing the limits of totalizing, universalist discourse and in recognizing the limitations or historical failures of the great "metanarratives" of liberalism and Marxism. If critique is to be "reconstructed," as Habermas wishes, reconstruction must be accomplished on the difficult terrain of a Nietzschean view of the truth.

To my mind, the most interesting effort to conserve traditional forms of (Marxist) critique is the work of Fredric Jameson, particularly in his attacks on poststructuralism. His treatment of poststructuralism is complex and ambivalent. From one side Jameson's Marxism has led him, like Anderson and Habermas, to condemn poststructuralism as counterrevolutionary. He characterizes Lyotard's *Postmodern Condition*, for example, as "indistinguishable from anti-Marxism."[37] Marxist analysis leads Jameson to regard poststructuralism as the ideology of a new, multinational stage of capitalism.[38] This political condemnation of poststructuralism, which comes from the mid-1980s, represents a change in his thinking. Earlier, in *The Political Unconscious*, Jameson was eager to incorporate the best features of poststructuralist thought within the wider framework of a totalizing Marxist position. In a grand gesture, he suggested that "Marxism subsumes other interpretive modes or systems . . . [but] the limits of the latter can always be overcome, and their more positive findings retained, by a radical historicizing of their mental operations."[39] But by 1984, when he completed the "radical historicizing of [poststructuralist] mental operations," Jameson's posture was the defensive exclusion of a dangerous ideological opponent.

From another side, as a reader of culture, Jameson presents the most coherent depictions of poststructuralism available. His immanent critiques of the phenomenon are brilliant examples of the genre. So cogently does he present poststructuralism that his texts make a compelling case for its importance and richness.[40] He treats poststructural-

[37]Jameson, "The Politics of Theory," p. 61.

[38]Fredric Jameson, "Postmodernism and Consumer Society," in Hal Foster, ed., *The Anti-Aesthetic: Essays on Postmodern Culture* (Port Townsend, Wash.: Bay Press, 1983), p. 125.

[39]Fredric Jameson, *The Political Unconscious: Narrative as a Socially Symbolic Act* (Ithaca: Cornell University Press, 1981), p. 47.

[40]This is especially so in "Postmodernism and Consumer Society," and in "Postmodernism; or, The Cultural Logic of Late Capitalism," *New Left Review* 146 (July–August 1984), 53–92.

ism as one side of postmodernism, stressing the relations between French theorists and primarily American cultural expressions in architecture, film, television, and so forth. He is careful to distance his position from the virulent attacks on recent culture by leftists such as Christopher Lasch.[41] With an almost loving brush he portrays the lines of an emergent cultural form as no one before him. His essays on postmodernism can be readily recommended to anyone who is curious about it.

From yet another side, Jameson presents the contemporary world as intelligible only from the point of view of poststructuralism. In this mode he openly admits the inadequacy of Marxism to comprehend the present conjuncture. The Marxist concept of ideology, he writes in Althusserian terms, explains the "gap" or "rift" between "existential experience and scientific knowledge." In our situation the concept of ideology no longer works. The radically new "space" of postmodernism, which undermines all efforts of self-location, of referential self-coordination, requires entirely new categories of thought, an "aesthetic of cognitive mapping" in order to achieve "a breakthrough to some as yet unimaginable new mode of representing . . . in which we may again begin to grasp our positioning as individual and collective subjects and regain a capacity to act and struggle which is at present neutralized by our spatial as well as our social confusion. The political form of postmodernism . . . will have as its vocation the invention and projection of a global cognitive mapping."[42] In rigorous honesty Jameson admits "confusion," acknowledges the inadequacy of Marxism, and calls upon poststructuralism, no longer viewed as an anti-Marxist "ideology," as the only hope for a reconstituted critical theory.

Holding all three positions in tense, ambivalent balance, Jameson opens a path, however narrow, to an accommodation with poststructuralism. Surely he and Habermas are correct to point out tendencies in that intellectual stance which are not conducive to critical social theory. But I would contend, in agreement with Jameson's third position, that poststructuralism contains some of the elements for the beginning of a critical analysis of the present. More particularly, certain of Foucault's positions clear away obstacles to an intellectual movement in that direction. These advances need to be outlined. After

---

[41]Jameson, "Cultural Logic of Late Capitalism," p. 71.
[42]Ibid., p. 92. See also "Cognitive Mapping," in *Marxism and the Interpretation of Culture*, ed. Cary Nelson and Lawrence Grossberg (Chicago: University of Illinois Press, 1988).

doing so, I will add my reservations about poststructuralism, along with suggestions for new strategies to supplement the strengths of the position.

First, Foucault, like many poststructuralists, cogently addresses the problem of the theoretical subject.[43] Since Descartes, theorists have assumed that a rational voice was also a universal one, that the theorist strove for rationality as the main trait of his or her theoreticity, that attaining such a position was equivalent to being able to speak for humanity, for every man, woman, and child on earth. The problem with this theoretical voice is not simply ethnocentricity but also that rational subjects of knowledge are now, in the advanced societies, in positions of power. Biologists, chemists, and physicists not only generate knowledge that is regarded as the highest form of truth; they are inserted into key positions in high-tech corporations, the military, and the government. Claims of the universality of reason may have always been epistemologically unfounded: today they are something worse than that, since reason is also the handmaid of institutions of unimaginably enormous force. Reason now legitimates and promotes institutions, both in the East and the West, whose only universality is their threat of total destruction.

The issue for theory, then, is to elaborate a position for the theoretical subject which acknowledges the contingency of its validity claims, the embeddedness of theory in the present, in the political conjuncture, without, however, relinquishing the critique of domination or the project of emancipation. In other words, the problem is to generate discourses whose power effects are limited as much as possible to the subversion of power. How such power effects will avoid legitimizing new powers is not at all clear. Habermas is right to see serious dangers of antirationalist conservatism and fascism in such an enterprise. The greater danger today may come not from those who shout "blood and soil" but from those who scientifically plan for war in the name of freedom. These are the people whose trigger fingers represent the culmination of Western reason.

Second, earlier theory posited a rational social subject, be it the bourgeois individual or the proletariat, as the reference point of freedom. Today theory must proceed without such stable signposts: if

---

[43]See especially Michel Foucault, "Truth and Power," in *Power/Knowledge: Selected Interviews and Other Writings, 1972–1977*, ed. Colin Gordon, trans. Colin Gordon et al. (New York: Pantheon, 1980), pp. 109–33.

there are social positions that are aligned with emancipation (women, gays, minorities), they are positions of oppression associated with marks of exclusion. Reason lies not with the oppressed but with the scientifically administered bureaucracies that are the agents of oppression. None of the oppressed groups can easily promise a free society as the outcome of their emancipation, as the long line of thinkers from Locke to Marx thought. Indeed, these movements often contain anti-emancipatory tendencies as well. In this conjuncture, Foucault generates his discourses about excluded terms (sex, insanity) and oppressed groups (prisoners) not as the solution to the riddle of history but as part of the problem. The texts of the critical theorist are discursive interventions in a field of contending forces that might be of assistance in clarifying the position of the oppressed. To the greatest extent possible they attempt to avoid taking possession of a hegemonic position within the movement, a fate that befell the discourse of Locke in 1776, Rousseau in 1789, and Marx in 1917 and 1949.

The intellectual's will to power is stashed in his or her text in the form of universal reason. The art of appropriating the universal was the main business of the Enlightenment. The philosophes were master impressionists whose collective textual voice ventriloquized that of humanity but spoke for a particular social class. Diderot elevated the philosophes' polemic into a morality. The captain of the Party of Humanity, Diderot wished most deeply for immortality in the memory of an emancipated mankind, although he had another, far more skeptical voice, as evidenced in *Rameau's Nephew*.[44] Still, the future of modern politics was mapped by the editor of the *Encyclopedia*: in generations to come, those who spoke for humanity automatically resurrected the saints of Enlightenment. By specifying the universal truth of the ideal speech situation, Habermas's text, echoing the Enlightenment, becomes the blueprint of freedom, his mind the noumenon of liberation. Foucault and the poststructuralists offer far less.

Third, the theorist constitutes him- or herself as textual agent through a critique of discursive practices that celebrate contemporary hegemonic institutions. For Baudrillard the target of criticism is the media; for Foucault it is the human sciences associated with the welfare state; for Derrida it is the Western philosophical tradition. The poststructuralist intervention endeavors to locate the place of power in

---

[44]Denis Diderot, "Encyclopedia," trans. Jacques Barzun in *Rameau's Nephew and Other Works* (New York: Bobbs-Merrill, 1964), p. 288 passim.

the discursive formation, to analyze how this power operates on the subject, and to elaborate strategies to reveal the play of that power. Habermas, instead, aims to locate the point where he can speak the truth, define its conditions, and plot the next stage of human emancipation accordingly. His goal is to outline a position against which one can only be defined as a counterrevolutionary. His strategy is that of Marx, Freud, and the Enlightenment: to oppose him is to be an enemy of mankind, *l'infame*, whose only fate is to be crushed. Habermas's strategy is one of totalization: to encompass the position of rational enlightenment to such an extent that all opponents are irrational.[45] The poststructuralist project is far more modest. It aims at a detotalized position that, finally, is uncertain of itself, a strategic intervention in an indeterminate field of forces whose outcome is contingent.

In one respect Habermas is right to be wary of the poststructuralists or at least of Foucault. So reluctant is Foucault to totalize his position that he avoids conceptual clarification and systematic argument to a fault. The consequence of his timidity is a failure of generality, of indicating the lines of force of his themes in the present, however much he orients his work to that end. To help rectify this weakness, I have proposed that the poststructuralist position be developed into a critical theory of the mode of information, a regional theory of new language situations characterized by electronic mediation.[46] I suggest that what Jameson terms our current spatial "confusion" may be due in part to the structurally new ways in which we are constituted as subjects in electronically mediated language formations. Television ads, data bases, and computers, to select some cogent examples, position the individual as a decentered, dispersed subject outside the binary oppositions of freedom/determinism, subject/object, identity/difference, thereby undermining the reference points of theory. If that is the case, domination is no longer only a question of (political and economic) action but also concerns discursive forms through which the subject is positioned in cultural space.

This presentation of the controversy between Habermas and the French poststructuralists is necessarily a fictional invention, since the

---

[45]There is a similar totalizing element in some of the positions of the poststructuralists. To the extent, for example, that deconstructionists discourage criticism of Derrida's position by charging the critic with logocentrism, they are setting a totalizing enclosure into place.

[46]See Mark Poster, *The Mode of Information* (New York: Blackwell, forthcoming).

actual relations between the two positions have not been extensively argued. The "debate" between German and French theory clarifies the issues for the further development of criticism in the age of the mode of information. Without abandoning the emancipatory aims of critical theory, as currently presented by Habermas, this further work will benefit from the criticisms of logocentrism enunciated by poststructuralists. In teasing out a position from the tangle of antagonisms between critical theory and poststructuralism, my aim, in subsequent chapters, will be to clarify the theoretical problems in relation to the context of the mode of information.

2

Sartre's Concept
of the Intellectual

The immediate postwar period (1944–1947) is generally recognized as a time of great expectations for social progress, even revolution. With fascism defeated and the Right largely discredited, Western Europe looked forward to a period of democratic rebuilding and renewal. In France, perhaps more than elsewhere, these hopes were supported by a substantial left-wing majority in government. Leftist intellectuals, who had participated to varying degrees in the Resistance movement, shared the sanguine spirit of the time. In particular some of the major existentialists—Jean-Paul Sartre, Maurice Merleau-Ponty, and Simone de Beauvoir—were strongly taken by the mood of optimism, a fact that might surprise those who view their philosophy as one of despair, anguish, and melancholy. In 1944 the existentialists were fully convinced that they could make important contributions to the movement toward social freedom.[1] The widespread success of existentialist thought in these years served to convince Sartre and his friends that their ideas might have a prominent role in shaping the political future of France and Europe.

In fact, things did not turn out as expected either for France or for the existentialists. Sartre quickly became embroiled in controversies with his erstwhile allies and friends, the Communists. In the press and on the radio existentialism became subject to scandal and smear tac-

[1]See, for example, Jean-Paul Sartre, "A propos de l'existentialisme, mise au point," *Action* 17 (1944), 11.

tics.[2] Liberals such as Albert Camus and Raymond Aron also became estranged from the existentialists. It did not take long before the alliances forged during the struggle against fascism dissolved into bitter and enduring enmities. To make matters worse, those who were devoted to existentialism were often not the sort of people Sartre aspired to impress. Although opinions evolved quickly during these years, it was a time more conducive to frantic activity and frustrated hopes than to solid advances.

One of the central problems for Sartre and his group during the mid-1940s was to define the work of intellectuals. The events of the war years had so drastically transformed the lives of philosophers, novelists, and scholars that they could not easily return to the quiet study, the contemplation of eternal questions of being, or the crafting of an artistic object that spoke only to itself. Nor was it easy, as Julien Benda had a generation earlier,[3] to claim for intellectuals a privileged status that allowed them to stand back from the world and speak down to it as a teacher to pupils, condemning this and praising that, according to the dictates of reason. On the other hand, engagement in the world also contained its share of snares and false promises. A number of intellectuals had rushed into the Communist party, assured of a direct connection with the progressive social forces. But many of them soon found that the tools of the critical intellect were useless in a shop that produced justifications for pragmatic action rather than theories to guide it. Thus the situation for the existentialists was not unambiguous: on the right, outmoded notions of purity and transcendence; on the left, compromising subservience to opportunistic political parties. Yet one had to choose. So the existentialists opted to forge a new kind of weapon out of the materials of intellectual life, one that would preserve the virtues of reflection and literature while fully engaging in the whirl of history.

Looking back at the predicament of the existentialists and the conclusions they drew about the role of intellectuals, one can distinguish

[2]For an account of the trials and hopes of the existentialists during this period, see Simone de Beauvoir, *Force of Circumstance*, trans. Richard Howard (New York: Putnam's, 1964). Also useful are Michel-Antoine Burnier, *Choice of Action*, trans. Bernard Murchland (New York: Vintage, 1968); David Caute, *Communism and the French Intellectuals, 1914–1960* (New York: Macmillan, 1964); and Mark Poster, *Existential Marxism in Postwar France* (Princeton: Princeton University Press, 1976). See B. D. Graham, *The French Socialists and Tripartisme, 1944–1947* (Toronto: Toronto University Press, 1965), for the general political situation.

[3]Julien Benda, *La trahison des clercs* (Paris: Grasset, 1927).

not only the innovative figure of engagement but also certain deeply rooted continuities with the past. Michel Foucault's criticisms of earlier generations of intellectuals enable us to consider afresh the posture of the existentialists and to elaborate a more nuanced analysis of the limitations of their notion of intellectual life. In this chapter I adopt the vantage point outlined by Foucault to reexamine the definition of the intellectual put forward by the existentialists during the years from 1944 to 1947. In particular I hold the Foucauldian lens up to the major work on the topic of intellectuals: Sartre's *What Is Literature?*

From the 1950s to the present France has, it can be argued, experienced three distinct periods of intellectual activity. Until the early 1960s, discussion was dominated by a developing synthesis of Marxism and existentialism which I have termed existential Marxism. In the mid-1960s, structuralism came to the fore. Both of these intellectual currents were characterized by a strong totalizing impulse, a tendency toward systemization, and by the profoundly held assumption that reason was adequate to the comprehension of reality. In the 1970s came a third period, that of poststructuralism, which reversed the earlier trends quite drastically. In the hands of Jacques Derrida and Michel Foucault, the most arresting poststructuralists, the potential scope and claims of reason were sharply curtailed. Derrida attacked what he called the Western philosophical tradition for its logocentrism, the assertion of the immediacy of reality to thought, and the assumption of the ability of reason to represent reality.[4] In a similar but separate vein, Foucault argued, notably in *Les mots et les choses*, that the limits of discourse were undermined by underlying epistemological constraints that were outside and beneath the ken of their authors.[5] In both instances poststructuralism drew attention to the impasses and errors incurred when the inevitable limitations of the scope of reason were transgressed.

In 1979 Foucault expanded his critique of reason to include the role of the intellectuals. He was extremely critical of the traditional pretension of the intellectual, the claim that he or she alone can represent the universal. With Voltaire and Sartre in mind, Foucault characterized the intellectual: "For a long time the 'left' intellectual spoke and was acknowledged to have the right of speaking in the capacity of master

---

[4]Jacques Derrida, *Of Grammatology*, trans. Gayatri Spivak (Baltimore: Johns Hopkins University Press, 1974).
[5]Michel Foucault, *Les mots et les choses*, trans. as *The Order of Things: An Archaeology of the Human Sciences* (New York: Pantheon, 1970).

of truth and justice."[6] Armed with the lance of reason and the sword of the written word, the intellectual presented him- or herself as a crusader for universality, a grasp of which would enable the intellectual alone to win the battle of progress. The difficulties that ensue from this "universal intellectual," Foucault contends, are all too evident in the history of Marxism. The proletariat, a historically constituted, finite social group, initially has universality attributed to it, only to have it promptly stolen by the intellectual, who now claims the consciousness of this universality. The theorist or party leader can speak for the proletariat in the name of a universality that is somehow lost amid the grime of the process of production. In this way the intellectual's assertion of universality easily becomes an alibi for grasping power; knowledge and power are locked in a misalliance that can be traced back to Plato's philosopher-king.

Foucault discerns a trend, however, beginning after World War II, which rejects the universal intellectual in favor of a figure he terms the specific intellectual. With Robert Oppenheimer representing the point of transition, the specific intellectual no longer claims *to speak for* another group or to give voice to an oppressed consciousness. The role of the specific intellectual is rather to facilitate, for a subordinate social group, its ability to speak for itself. The specific intellectual represents nothing and no one; he or she enables the oppressed to name themselves and write their own *cahiers de doléances*. In addition, the specific intellectual is not "the man of justice" who floats above society, alert to its inequities, ready to denounce the atrocities of capitalism and to put them in a universal perspective. Instead, the specific intellectual is rooted in a particular institution. From a position in, and knowledge of, that institution he or she may speak about its structure of domination without claiming more than his or her due.

In outlining the distinction between universal and specific intellectuals, Foucault does not analyze the social conditions that bring the latter on the scene. He does not mention changes in the structure of the capitalist mode of production which spread intellectual functions throughout society, in the factory, the government bureau, the welfare agency, the hospital, even the military. Nor does he redefine in any satisfactory way the role of the intellectual as intellectual, at least

[6]Michel Foucault, "Truth and Power," in *Working Papers*, ed. Meaghan Morris and Paul Patton (Sydney: Ferral Publications, 1979), p. 41. This piece is also available in Michel Foucault, *Power/Knowledge: Selected Interviews and Other Writings*, ed. Colin Gordon (New York: Pantheon, 1980).

not in the 1970s, when he outlined the distinction between the universal and the specific intellectual. Despite these limitations, I believe that Foucault's distinction is important and that it can serve to identify difficulties in the existentialist definition of the intellectual in the immediate postwar years.

In 1947 Sartre wrote a series of articles which appeared in *Les Temps Modernes* and were later collected and published as *What Is Literature?* In light of the recent devastating war and the current hopes for large-scale social change, Sartre reconsidered the nature of writing and the role of the intellectual in history. The term *literature* in the title of the essay was used in the broad eighteenth-century sense to include philosophy, history, and literature. It was apparent to Sartre that one could no longer ignore history, that one could no longer write and think in a philosophical and aesthetic vacuum. Because the intellectual had been engulfed by the activities of war, it was now essential to conceive of writing as action. "Thus the prose writer is a man who has chosen a certain method of secondary action which we may call action by disclosure."[7] The intellectual committed to writing as a form of action in the world was said to be *engagé*, a term that became the catchword for a generation of intellectuals throughout the West.

The notion that intellectuals do not simply interpret the world but act upon it and change it is associated with the writings of Karl Marx, specifically with the eleventh thesis on Ludwig Feuerbach. Sartre, however, held that the notion of the engaged writer derived equally from his own brand of existentialism. In *What Is Literature?* he couched his argument in the philosophical phrases not of Marx but of *Being and Nothingness*. Writing is a form of doing and "doing reveals being. Each gesture traces out new forms on the earth. Each technique, each tool, is a way that opens upon the world; things have as many aspects as there are ways of using them. We are no longer with those who want to possess the world, but with those who want to change it" (165). The existentialist writer must therefore "plunge things into action" and develop a form of literature which has as its singular aim that of "making history," eschewing the literature of *exis* (passivity) for that of *praxis*.

Although the engaged writer was a child of existentialism, Sartre was not satisfied with his writings of the thirties. The contemplative

---

[7]Jean-Paul Sartre, *What Is Literature?* trans. Bernard Frechtman (New York: Washington Square Press, 1966), p. 14, hereafter cited parenthetically in the text.

musings of Roquentin in *Nausea* were rejected as a model for the protagonist in *Paths of Freedom*. The purely philosophical stance Sartre took in *The Transcendence of the Ego, L'Imaginaire,* and *Being and Nothingness* he thereafter rejected in favor of more politically motivated writing such as one finds in *Critique of Dialectical Reason*. Furthermore, after 1947 Sartre sought an appropriate form of political action. A consistent political thread runs through his activities, from the Rassemblement Démocratique Révolutionnaire of 1948 through the years of fellow traveling with the Communist party down to May 1968 and the support he gave to Maoists by selling their newspapers in the street. In each case Sartre was attempting to fulfill the program of *What Is Literature?* or, as he later put it, to transform a leftist intellectual into an intellectual leftist. The success or wisdom of Sartre's politics may be debated, but one cannot doubt the consistency of the effort.

Sartre also relied on the philosophical positions of *Being and Nothingness* in outlining the character of the engaged intellectual's contribution to history. Freedom was the central concept in defining the role of the writer. For Sartre human beings were free because consciousness is a lack, an opening to the world that no object can determine. This freedom gave human beings the opportunity to make themselves, and more particularly, it was the basis for the intellectual's opportunity to have an effect on the world. The writer of literature transcended the given and in so doing challenged it. He held up against the given a world of facticity, containing possibilities the reader could recognize, yet which could awaken his sense of freedom. "Literature," Sartre maintained, "is the work of a total freedom addressing plenary freedoms and thus in its own way manifests the totality of the human condition as a free product of a creative activity. . . . Every day we must take sides; in our life as a writer, in our articles, in our books. Let it always be by preserving as our guiding principle the rights of total freedom as an effective synthesis of formal and material freedoms. Let this freedom manifest itself in our novels, our essays, and our plays. And if our characters do not yet enjoy it, if they live in our time, let us at least be able to show what it costs them not to have it" (192). Anything but an aesthetic activity, literature was to be the gadfly of existential freedom, urging the reader, perhaps against his or her will, to recognize oppression, envisage authenticity, and struggle for revolution.

Although Sartre viewed literature as an appeal to the freedom of the reader, he was realistic enough to discern that many obstacles stood between the author's freedom as embodied in a work of fiction and the reader's freedom. The chief obstacle in 1947, according to Sartre, was the class structure of society. The realization of the freedom projected in literature was only possible in a classless society. In such a world, where toil and oppression were not disproportionately imposed on one group at the expense of another, the fortunate writer would find that his or her subject matter was closely related to the perspectives of the whole society. Although literature, according to Sartre, always dwelled upon man as a being-in-the-world, the actual reading public was a far more restricted group than the general public or than society at large. This disparity had been the condition for a possible confusion in which "the interests and cares of man" are taken to be "those of a small and favored group" (105–6).

It is of course, debatable whether "man in the world" is the only subject of literature. Many would argue, for example, that language is the only subject of literature. Still, Sartre's position is clear: in a class society the writer identifies only with certain groups, capturing the totality from the vantage point of those groups. A bourgeois writer writes from a bourgeois perspective, depicting workers only as the bourgeois sees them. That is clear enough in a monarchist like Balzac, a bourgeois like Flaubert, and a democrat like Zola. The consequence of this partiality is that the relation of freedom to freedom is broken as ideology betrays the voice of freedom. In a classless society, on the contrary, the writer defends the interests of all. Under these circumstances, Sartre insists,

the writer will renew it [the world] as is, the raw, sweaty, smelly, everyday world, in order to submit it to freedoms on the foundation of a freedom. Literature in this classless society would thus be the world aware of itself, suspended in a free act, and offering itself to the free judgment of all men, the reflective self-awareness of a classless society. It is by means of the book that the members of this society would be able to get their bearings, see themselves and their situation. [107]

Sartre's understanding or vision of the writer in a classless society conforms to the definition of the universal intellectual as Foucault has sketched it. The writer speaks for everyone. The writer is the great representative of humanity's freedom. The voice of the writer, and only that voice it would seem, can utter the words of freedom. The writer's pen can transcribe in the book the needs and aspirations of every individual. The writer's imagination can invent the figures that confront everyone with the potential for freedom, the aspiration to authenticity. Thus Sartre perpetuates, at least in his dream of the perfect writer in the perfect world, the prejudice against partiality, the critique of factions, and the doctrines of natural rights and universal reason, stances originating in the Enlightenment and culminating in Hegel's identification of truth with totality.

Surveying the situation in 1947, Sartre recognized clearly enough that the social conditions of writing were not those of the existentialist or Marxist utopia. Society was indeed divided into classes, sharply restricting the public available to the writer. The question that confronted the engaged writer, therefore, was how to acknowledge the prevailing social conditions and still allow space for his own influence. Sartre attempted a dialectical formulation of the problem in which the writer and the public entered into a reciprocal interaction that was effective but not completely determining. "One cannot write without a public and without a myth—without a *certain* public which historical circumstances have made, without a *certain* myth of literature which depends to a very great extent upon the demand of this public. In a word, the author is in a situation, like all other men. But his writings, like every human project, simultaneously enclose, specify, and surpass this situation" (101). The writer was thus faced with the obstacle of an unfree situation, which was, paradoxically, a condition for the exercise of freedom.

On the more concrete level of the particular circumstances of the postwar period in France, Sartre was compelled to acknowledge that things were bleak indeed. The situation might be necessary for freedom, but Sartre's situation, as he understood it, did not offer much prospect for the realization of the literature of praxis. The first harsh condition imposed by the situation of a class society on the writer was, Sartre stoically pronounced, that the writer was bourgeois and the public was not. After a short sketch of the history of literature since the nineteenth century, Sartre was forced to admit the bourgeois nature of literary production. "That's what we are. In other respects, saints, heroes, mystics, adventurers, angels, enchanters, executioners, victims, as you like. But, first of all, bourgeois" (113).

Just as the writer was bourgeois, so were the readers, a second unwanted feature of the situation in 1947. No sophisticated statistical analysis of book sales was required to demonstrate that the people who bought Sartre's books, who subscribed to *Les Temps Modernes*, who followed the arguments of the intellectuals in the periodicals were very much the same people who had a dominant position in the relations of production. Although this was the fact for writers in general, it seemed particularly valid with respect to Sartre. Postwar existentialism simply did not appeal to what Sartre considered the progressive social forces. What was worse, perhaps, was the charge by Communist intellectuals that those marginal groups who might turn to the party were drifting away from it toward existentialism. The young bourgeois who rejected the life of his parents and was open, at least potentially, to the appeal of the cause of Marxism was instead devouring the message of the existentialists and choosing individualist solutions. Sartre was more than a little perturbed by these accusations, but he had no effective answer to them. All he could do was to point to his own experience in World War II. The individualist project of authenticity—the message of his earlier writings—was inappropriate to the situation: "Our life as an individual which had seemed to depend upon our efforts, our virtues, and our faults, on our good and bad luck, on the good and bad will of a very small number of people, seemed governed down to its minutest details by obscure and collective forces, and its most private circumstances seemed to reflect the state of the whole world. All at once we felt ourselves abruptly situated" (147). Though the force of circumstances was compelling enough to Sartre and his friends, the younger generation scandalously preferred to ignore it.

When Sartre analyzed the situation of the writer in 1947 more closely, he came upon still greater obstacles. There was still the proletariat to appeal to: "We turn toward the working class which today, like the bourgeoisie in 1789, might constitute for the writer a revolutionary public" (174). Even if this rather simplistic analogy between 1947 and 1789 were appropriate, there was no reason to suspect that the working class would listen to Sartre. But he persisted. The existentialist rejected the Communist party's heroic myth of the proletariat while accepting its importance in history. Therefore the conclusion was inevitable: "It must be said without hesitation that the fate of literature is bound up with that of the working class" (175). So much the worse, for the distressing reality was that the working class, or so Sartre thought, was sequestered under the ever-watchful gaze of the party. A bourgeois intellectual, associated in the eyes of the party with the demimonde of Paris, could never break through the curtain of propaganda with which the Communists enshrouded him. With frustration and pathos Sartre wrote, "Unhappily, these men, to whom we *must* speak, are separated from us by an iron curtain in our own country; they will not hear a word that we shall say to them. The majority of the proletariat, straight-jacketed by a single party . . . forms a closed society without doors or windows. There is only one way of access, a very narrow one, the Communist Party" (175).

In this situation Sartre was faced with an unpalatable choice: join the party and gain access to the workers but surrender all independence, or remain outside the party and write for the bourgeoisie. Since the first alternative was impossible, he took his chances with the second. As a result, Sartre, perhaps the most famous writer of his day, had "readers but no public." Incredible as it sounds, the existentialist writer insisted that he had no audience, at least none he was willing to recognize as his own. But this predicament only strengthened Sartre's will. The challenge of the situation evoked a still greater determination to overcome the obstacles. In a sense proving his own thesis that the situation could be overcome by freedom, Sartre resolved to create his own public where none existed. Picturing himself as the underdog David in a death struggle with Goliath, Sartre wrote, "Our engagement must begin the moment we are repulsed and excommunicated by the Churches, when the art of writing, wedged in between different propagandas, seems to have lost its characteristic effectiveness" (184). At this dramatic moment in his literary career, when all odds seemed against him, Sartre developed a strategy for combat in which there were certain assumptions concerning the nature of the intellectual, which betray the revolutionary posture he wished to adopt and which are central to the conclusions of this chapter.

In *What Is Literature?* Sartre outlined a program, consisting of three main proposals, by which he would fulfill the image of the engaged writer in the situation of 1947. The first task was the realistic assessment of the audience, those groups that could not be reached (workers, peasants, Christians) and those that potentially could be reached. It is worth noting that Sartre did not mention those groups he had already reached, an omission that lends support to his detractors, who denounced the followers of existentialism as social trash. Sartre's "virtual readers," the group he would now win over, were certain uncommitted sections of the petite bourgeoisie—teachers and "those popular factions which have not joined up with communism" (185). The appeal to the petite bourgeoisie as a potential source of radicalism is more astute than it might appear. Within Marxist circles a debate has flourished for some time concerning the role of the petite bourgeoisie in social revolution, which clearly suggests the wisdom of addressing their concerns.[8] The first step in Sartre's program was eminently logical.

Next Sartre searched for a means to reach his virtual reader. In addition to the book, which Sartre thought only reached the bourgeoisie, he would turn to the mass media—radio, newspapers, and films. It was not a question of popularization, Sartre insisted, but of communicating to people in ways that could be heard. The mass media had opened new avenues for the exchange of ideas, and it did not matter that they were not often used for this purpose. At age forty-two, Sartre was still sensitive enough to his surroundings to realize the importance of the mass media. He had recognized that the committed intellectual could, in the mid–twentieth century, escape from the traditional confines of politico-philosophical discourse. From the 1940s until his death, Sartre made numerous efforts to employ the new media, including television, in order to spread his ideas. Doubtless he also enjoyed the attention the media gave him, becoming something of an intellectual star. It is surprising that he was seemingly oblivious to the dangers inherent in electronic publicity. Just as he regarded language as nothing more than a tool for the expression of conscious thoughts and feelings, so too he ignored the alienating effects of the media, the ways in which the structure of the media inserts its own meanings into communication regardless of the motives of the person being broadcast or televised.

The crucial issue for Sartre remained how to transform a disparate audience into a public, "an organic unity of readers, listeners and spectators" (187). Only as a public, Sartre thought, could his audience change from passivity and isolation to a collective solidarity and political effectiveness. The argument Sartre presented for creating a public reveals, I think, his limitations as a universal intellectual. At the outset Sartre betrays his allegiance to the typical myth of the intellectual "The man who reads . . . ," he claims, "puts himself at the peak of his freedom" (187). (One has to assume that listening and watching are also included.) Sartre has retreated to the Enlightenment distinction between thought and action. In the act of quiet reflection one is free; out in the world, one is subject to determining forces. Reading is a transcendental act beyond the constraining pressures of the Newto-

---

[8]See, for example, Jonathan Wiener, "Marxism and the Petty Bourgeoisie: A Reply to Arno Mayer," *Journal of Modern History* 48 (1976), 666–71.

nian world of nature. Sartre writes, "Thus, by his very exigence, the reader attains that chorus of good wills which Kant has called the City of Ends" (188). The reading audience is a community of free subjects bound together by the strongest and most sublime spiritual ties. Still, this community of free readers is not a public, not a force of historical change. In order for it to become so, two further conditions must be met: first, the reader must have an intuition of solidarity with others, and second, the community of good wills must become a real community. "These abstract good wills [must] establish real relations among themselves when actual events take place" (190).

Even if we grant Sartre the dubious claim about the freedom of the reader, we cannot go along with his next step: the assertion that the author can transform the spiritual community into a real one. For it is here that Sartre states explicitly, more explicitly than I have seen elsewhere, the fundamental assumption of the universal intellectual. "It is up to us," he writes, "to convert the city of ends into a concrete and open society—and this by the very content of our words" (190). There is no ambiguity, no embarrassment, no hesitation in Sartre's maneuver: the writer creates the public; the intellectual fashions the revolutionary mass; ideas, in short, shape reality. The action the intellectual takes represents nothing less than a royal command to the audience. Sartre proclaims himself philosopher-king without the need to hold office. The most sanctified value of Western civilization is announced without a shred of recognition of its historical limitations: knowledge is power.

The obvious contradiction of Sartre's position goes unperceived: he wants free readers to create a free world; he condemns the Communist party and the church as external forces aborting freedom; yet he places himself in the same position with respect to his readers as they have to theirs. Sartre acts upon his readers the same way they act on their followers. "If we start with the moral exigence which the aesthetic feeling envelops without meaning to do so, we are starting on the right foot. We must *historicize* the reader's good will, that is, by the formal agency of our work, we must, if possible, provoke his intention of treating men, in every case, as an absolute end and, by the *subject* of our writing, direct his intention upon his neighbors, that is, upon the oppressed of the world" (190). Sartre would play the role of God vis-à-vis his readers, determining their thoughts, changing their wills, yet allowing them to be free, indeed forcing them to create a free world. Quite an act of metaphysical acrobatics. In *Les aventures de la dialectique*

Merleau-Ponty traced Sartre's effort to determine the will of the reader/other to his reliance on the *cogito*, on his failure to relate the "I think" to the sensible, visible world, and therefore to his tendency to avoid the cruical mediations between self and other which might restrain the role accorded to the writer.[9]

The phrases Sartre employs to speak of his relation to his public manifest the power of the intellectual: the reader "will be led by the hand until he is made to see" (191); "we must remind them," "let us show them," "let us point out," "let us teach them" (202). For one sensitive to the least nuances of language, Sartre pays little heed to the manner in which he addresses free subjects. In one respect he can bemoan that "we are living in the age of mystifications" (197), that language has become seriously corrupted. "Our first duty as a writer," he insists, "is thus to re-establish language in its dignity. After all, we think with words" (197). The writer must not flinch, in an age of lies and duplicities, of cover-ups and alibis, from calling things by their names, from speaking the truth in all its plainness, whatever the consequences may be. Yet in another aspect Sartre imagines that he can establish a revolutionary public by decree, that he can hold up the banner of freedom by the force of his words.

The apparent contradiction in Sartre's position is explained by the assumption he holds about the nature of the intellectual. Although he maintains that all individuals are ontologically or potentially free, he writes as though only the intellectual were in fact free. Sartre takes it for granted that the truth is available to him alone and yet that this truth applies to all. Only on this basis is it possible for him to maintain that he knows the needs of his readers better than they themselves. "Our job is to reveal to the public its own needs" (186) is a statement whose arrogance requires no elaboration. As is typical of the universal intellectual, Sartre does not even find it necessary to justify the privileged position of the intellectual. The arrogation of truth to the writer comes naturally and is not open to argument. Perhaps there is a remnant of patriarchy here: just as the father knows the needs of the child better than the child does, so the intellectual knows best the needs of the public.

In the end it is a matter of whose voice will be heard. Sartre thinks that his voice can stand in place of his audience, can represent it. "Our

[9]Maurice Merleau-Ponty, *Les aventures de la dialectique* (Paris: Gallimard, 1955), pp. 261–67.

job as a writer is to represent the world and to bear witness to it" (199). The intellectual thus stands in the place of the audience, thinking and speaking for it. One can argue about whether this system is Leninist or bourgeois, democratic centralist or parliamentary. The Sartrean intellectual is Leninist in that the voice that speaks the truth or holds the proper theoretical position naturally assumes the mantle of power. But he is bourgeois in that he has won his audience in the marketplace of ideas, through a competition with others which is a kind of election.

The analysis of the concept of the intellectual in *What Is Literature?* leads to the conclusion that Sartre's assumptions about the writer do indeed fit into the category of the universal intellectual as outlined by Foucault. The dangers inherent in such a definition of the writer are severe and work against the ideological ambitions of the engaged intellectual. Sartre, of course, did not presume to speak for the whole of society, just for the petite bourgeoisie, or an important section of it. Yet he laid the basis for his relation to that audience in the utopia of a classless society in which the intellectual would finally become universal. That utopia crept back into his sociologically realistic analysis of the situation in 1947 in the sense that Sartre's relation to his limited audience was couched in the same representational form it would take in the classless world. In 1947 Sartre estimated that he could command the voices of only one group, while in the future he might speak for everyone.

The difficulty in this position, as Foucault sees it, is twofold: first, there is no justification, epistemological or otherwise, for the representationality of the intellectual; second, in this arrangement, since the popular forces never get the opportunity to speak, one never knows if pronouncements of the intellectual are indeed correct or not. With regard to the first problem, a politically retrograde notion of truth is fostered: there is one truth and it is controlled by those who best manipulate logic and language.[10] With regard to the second problem, the masses are led to rely on the propositions of an external voice that can easily misrepresent them. Worse yet, in this form of intellectual practice, the masses do not develop the habit of speaking for themselves, of developing discourses that relate to their practice. The absolute separation of discourse and practice is maintained or, better, a specialization of functions is established by which discourse emerges

---

[10]See David Carroll, "The Subject of Archaeology or the Sovereignty of the Episteme," *Modern Language Notes* 93 (1978), 695, 722.

at one point in the field of forces and practice at another, a non-synchronous politics whose faults are well exemplified in both the bourgeois and the Communist camps.

Foucault, like Sartre, connects knowledge and power, intellect and will, but in a manner that undercuts the Sartrean universal intellectual in favor of the specific intellectual. He does this by shifting the level of analysis to situations in daily life in which the intellectual function is closely bound in practice to the audience. He seeks those places in society where discourse is implicated in action: the hospital staff with its doctors; the welfare agency with its social service workers; the military with its scientific and technical cadres; the prison with its criminologists and legal experts. In these instances discourse and practice are mingled, each is constrained by the other. The intellect does not act upon the will as from outside but is always already formed by it. Foucault sees no privileged place of freedom where knowledge becomes a general power. The specific intellectual cannot fabricate an "open society," to use Sartre's words, but only expose the pattern of domination inherent in a particular institution.

Foucault's critique of the universal intellectual has much to say for itself. It undermines, in a Nietzchean fashion, the traditional Western assumptions about truth, writing, and the philosopher. It opens up the question of the relation of theory to practice in a manner that has not been seen since the days of Marx. Foucault decenters and multiplies the locus of theory or discourse, upsetting an easy reconciliation with politics or the class struggle. At neither end of the dichotomy between theory and practice is there a simple resolution. The intellectual is not the universal theorist; the proletariat is not the universal revolutionary force. At the same time, there is a *practice* in the theory of the intellectuals, and there is a *theory* in the practice of progressive social forces. Foucault's position is certainly a refreshing reformulation of issues that long remained stagnant and uncompelling.

Nevertheless there are dangers in Foucault's position, the most obvious of which is the credence it seems to lend to a problematic form of pluralism. If the intellectual is proscribed from theorizing the totality, consigned instead to the boundaries of local institutions, then political protest, it would appear, must also remain confined to individual issues, local affairs, interest-group pressures. General social transformation has apparently been abandoned in favor of a guerrilla warfare of structural reforms. If the dangers of representing the totality are so great that no one may speak for society, there arises the implication that everyone has something to say about their limited circumstances. If there is no general Truth and no general Politics, then all particular truth and all particular politics are sanctioned. Foucault, of course, did not maintain this position or even concede validity to it. Yet he did not clarify his position on pluralism, lending it a sort of silent approval.

Pluralism can also be closely related to anarchism. The critique of the general intellectual goes arm in arm with a rejection of general politics. On many occasions Foucault spoke against the traditional assumption that power emanates from the central state. In its place he posited a multicentered view of power, in which power is dispersed throughout the social field in the smallest corners of everyday life. When power is conceived this way, the struggle against domination takes on a new pattern. The goal becomes a generalized assault on "the micro-physics of power." Such a view of politics goes along with the notion of the specific intellectual, but it also suggests an anarchist position in which society is ruled at once by no one and by everyone. The difficulty that must be faced, however, is that if domination is everywhere in daily life, the struggle against it seems hopeless.[11] Nothing prevents new forms of domination from replacing old ones, the new ills perhaps exceeding the old.

The second danger in Foucault's position is a logical one. The universal intellectual can be criticized only by a stance that itself is at some level universal. Foucault legislates in favor of the specific intellectual, the writer organically connected with an institution and group. Yet, the negation he posits is universal. Anyone who maintains the stance of the universal is subject to the representational fallacy, but to attack this "anyone" requires a universal statement. Foucault himself represents the totality when he denounces totalizing positions. Only by stepping beyond the limits of the specific intellectual can Foucault proclaim his universal theory in its favor. In sum, Foucault's statements about the universal intellectual are themselves universal, and his theory of the specific intellectual is a *general* theory of the intellectual. I do not think there is any way around this aporia, but it cannot be dismissed as a logical oddity without material effects.

By denying that general theory is possible or that general theory is truly revolutionary, Foucault is implicitly totalizing the situation. Taking a position against totalization, he incurs a totalizing statement.

[11]Jean Baudrillard makes this criticism in *Oublier Foucault* (Paris: Galilée, 1977).

Foucault needed to develop an epistemology and sociology of the intellectual which would account for the position of the critique of the universal intellectual. The question that needs to be raised, which Foucault did not raise, is "under what conditions might the universal intellectual be rejected in favor of the specific intellectual?" One cannot avoid the problems of the universal intellectual simply by negating that figure.

Foucault's difficulty with this issue can be clarified in relation to his peculiar refusal to present his own authorial voice in personal terms. At the moment of his greatest recognition as an author, the occasion of his inaugural lecture ("The Discourse on Language") at the highly prestigious Collège de France, Foucault would have preferred to disappear and remain nameless, disappropriating his own voice: "I would really like to have slipped imperceptibly into this lecture, as into all the others I shall be delivering, perhaps, over the years ahead. . . . At the moment of speaking, I would like to have perceived a nameless voice, long preceding me, leaving me merely to enmesh myself in it, taking up its cadence, and to lodge myself, when no one was looking, in its interstices as if it had paused an instant, in suspense, to beckon to me."[12] Foucault desires an inaudible beginning to his discourse in order to avoid a certain "anxiety" that surrounds words. Since discourse and power are closely interlinked, words are the source of "conflicts, triumphs, injuries, dominations and enslavements." To begin a discourse is thus to enter into a political world.

Perhaps the constraints on the specific intellectual also provide an explanation for Foucault's reluctance to appear on the mass media. Unlike Sartre, who eagerly participated in radio and television shows, Foucault avoided such publicity whenever possible. He is far more aware than Sartre was of the profound effects of the media. When he wanted to assist prisoners in their protests against conditions in the jails in the early 1970s, he calculated his appearance at the demonstrations outside prisons so that the media would be attracted to the location and therefore would publicize the prisoners' demands. But he himself refused to speak in front of the cameras; only the prisoners must be heard; their voices, not that of the intellectual, must pronounce the list of complaints.

[12]Michel Foucault, "The Discourse on Language," in *The Archaeology of Knowledge and the Discourse on Language*, trans. A. M. Sheridan Smith (New York: Pantheon, 1972), p. 215.

The same urge for anonymity is found in the opening pages of *The Archaeology of Knowledge*, Foucault's major statement on methodology in the human sciences. Written shortly before "Discourse on Language," the *Archaeology* does not fully develop the relation between discourse and power. Consequently, discourse can be depicted as a means by which the intellectual conceals her- or himself from the powers that be. Foucault, addressing his reader directly, asks:

What, do you imagine that I would take so much trouble and so much pleasure in writing, do you think that I would keep so persistently to my task, if I were not preparing—with a rather shaky hand—a labyrinth into which I can venture, in which I can move my discourse, opening up underground passages, forcing it to go far from itself, finding overhangs that reduce and deform its itinerary, in which I can lose myself and appear at last to eyes that I will never have to meet again. I am no doubt not the only one who writes in order to have no face. Do not ask who I am and do not ask me to remain the same: leave it to our bureaucrats and our police to see that our papers are in order.[13]

Faceless or voiceless, Foucault preferred, it would seem, not to be noticed.

Although Foucault's impulse toward anonymity is the same in both cases, the more recent position creates a greater difficulty for his notion of the specific intellectual. Once a close relation between knowledge and power is posited, as it is in the "The Discourse on Language," the urge to aural oblivion, to impersonality, erases particularity in favor of universality. The specific intellectual, after all, is characterized by personal relation to the audience: the specific intellectual is not a distant representative but a close participant. By contrast, Sartre, the universal intellectual, the "voice of reason," appears to his audience only in the silence of reading, an impersonal, distant voice, a transcendental presence who brings the good news of freedom to the oppressed and confused masses. The critique of the Sartrean intellectual cannot be made in a nameless discourse that merely reproduces universality in another form. Instead, the specific intellectual would have to accept fully the burden of his own discourse/practice. Through the particularity of voice, the specific intellectual would avoid the pretense to universality that Foucault objects to but embraces as a cloaked disguise.

It is clear that much remains to be done in clarifying the implications

[13]Foucault, *Archaeology of Knowledge*, p. 17.

of Foucault's critique of the universal intellectual. Nonetheless, the critique does afford a perspective by which one can view the limitations of the existentialist concept of the writer. The conclusion is inevitable that postwar intellectuals like Sartre were far less revolutionary in their theory of the writer than they thought. Their search for a third way beyond Marxism and liberalism was less successful than they thought. The engaged writer was a true alternative neither to the party theorist nor to the Olympian mandarin. Still, in the next chapter I explore the question of the writer as universal or specific intellectual in relation to the concept of totalization or in relation to the concept of the constitution of the self of the writer. In that context certain strengths of Sartre's position emerge, and as a result, some directions for a reconstruction of Foucault's position open up.

3

Foucault and the Problem of Self-Constitution

The question of the subject or the self has been a central issue of contention for intellectual movements in the twentieth century. Psychoanalysis, surrealism, existentialism, structuralism, and most recently poststructuralism have sought to differentiate themselves from prevailing positions by putting into question their formulations of the self. The point of disagreement has to some extent been remarkably consistent: the position under attack is said to present a doctrine of the self that is too centered, too unified, too rationalist, in short, too Cartesian. The flight from the Cartesian position on the self is characterized by a cycle of repetition. The new position misrecognizes the one under attack as the Cartesian position. Structuralists identified existentialists as Cartesians, even though existentialists took their position by attacking neo-Kantians as Cartesians. From Sartre contra Brunschvicg to Lévi-Strauss contra Sartre to Derrida contra Lacan, the rush continues to the position of the decentered self.

In Foucault's case the issue of the decentered self becomes very complicated. His earliest works (a translation of Ludwig Binswanger's *Psychology and Mental Illness* and *Madness and Civilization*) contained definite existentialist themes. The authenticity of madness (a form of decentering) was defended against rationalist claims (a form of Cartesianism). With *The Order of Things* Foucault dramatically shifted to the structuralist position with pronouncements about the death of man, the end of the subject, and so forth. Without completely identifying with structuralism Foucault studied the limitations of rationalist sciences in works on asylums (*The Birth of the Clinic*) and prisons (*Discipline and Punish*). He brilliantly dissected what he called "technologies of power," authorized by the sciences of medicine and criminology. In these disciplines individual subjects became cases, ruled by the normalizing power of the Cartesian scientific gaze. Foucault questioned the centered, authorial, scientific subject, undermining its claims of transcendent objectivity by demonstrating the connection of science to power, the roots of truth in the soil of politics. Far from neutral statements of truth, the discourses of science emerge fully implicated in practices of domination. Foucault's strategy of dispersing the centered subject among discourses/practices that generate "technologies of power" continued through the 1970s and *The History of Sexuality*, volume 1, *The Will to Truth*.

When volumes 2 and 3 of *The History of Sexuality* appeared in 1984, shortly before his death, Foucault's problematic of the self had considerably shifted. From the dispersal of the subject in discourse he moved to the issue of the "constitution of the self" in discourse. A centered self once again became a possibility, only now the self was understood in historical-social, not ontological terms. Position 1, of the 1960s (which Foucault was later to call archaeology), was a critique of the self as rationalist by a strategy of *reversal*: madness vs. reason. Position 2, of the 1970s (which Foucault was to call genealogy), was a critique of the self as centered consciousness by a strategy of *displacement*: the locus of intelligibility shifted from subject to structure. Position 3, of the 1980s (which Foucault was to call ethics), was a hermeneutics of the self using a strategy of *historicism*: the emphasis fell to the activity of self-constitution in discursive practices.[1]

In the last phase of Foucault's theory of the subject one senses a return of sorts to the problematic of Sartre and the existentialists. In

[1]There are a number of interesting studies of Foucault's intellectual career, each interpreting it somewhat differently. Here are some suggestions: Charles Lemert and Garth Gillan, *Michel Foucault: Social Theory as Transgression* (New York: Columbia University Press, 1982); Pamela Major-Poetzl, *Michel Foucault's Archaeology of Western Culture* (Chapel Hill: University of North Carolina Press, 1983); Hubert Dreyfus and Paul Rabinow, *Michel Foucault: Beyond Structuralism and Hermeneutics* (Chicago: University of Chicago Press, 1982); Barry Smart, *Foucault, Marxism, and Critique* (London: Routledge and Kegan Paul, 1983); John Rajchman, *Michel Foucault: The Freedom of Philosophy* (New York, Columbia University Press, 1985); Mark Cousins and Althar Hussain, *Michel Foucault* (New York: St. Martin's Press, 1984); Karlis Racevskis, *Michel Foucault and the Subversion of Intellect* (Ithaca: Cornell University Press, 1983); Mark Poster, *Foucault, Marxism, and History* (New York: Blackwell, 1985).

place of the hermeneutic of suspicion in Positions 1 and 2 there is an affirmative effort to comprehend a process of self-constitution, a genuine search for an ethics. In *Being and Nothingness* (1943) and *Critique of Dialectical Reason* (1960) Sartre carried out a similar quest. The existential Marxist attempted to locate a ground for the freedom of self-creation or, in Foucault's terms, self-constitution. Sartre's project was both a decentering and a recentering of the subject.[2] In *Being and Nothingness* self-creation was centered in the capacity to give meaning, which is very similar to Nietzsche's concept of values created by the will to power of the individual. Sartre associated the capacity of self-creation with time, nothingness, contingency, ex-centricity, alterity— all the negative attributes of the human condition as defined by what is now called the Western philosophical tradition. Sartre's reversal of that tradition recentered the subject in the most ephemeral aspects of being, which, at the same time, claimed to be more primordial and to exist at a deeper level of the self than Platonic reason. Sartrean freedom, developed in *Being and Nothingness* and extended in *Critique of Dialectical Reason*, was the theological power of the creation of the self *ex nihilo*.

From the vantage point of Foucault's Position 3 there is one chief difficulty with Sartre's position: it claims to define self-constitution for all humanity. Sartre's texts operate at the ontological level, sketching the contours of *l'être humain* with the indelible ink of the philosopher, the absolute author, the universal intellectual. In this sense an important part of the rationalist tradition is preserved and reinforced in the pages of the existentialist. Reason is reestablished as the ground of truth in Sartre's discourse because the manifesto of freedom in finitude is made from the absolute pulpit of the philosophical subject. Sartre both asserts the situated, limited nature of meaning, the particularity of self-creation, and speaks from the transcendent, unlimited locus of reason. Everything in *Being and Nothingness* works to give the impression that the truth it enunciates is absolute—or so, at least, things appeared to Foucault.

In the 1960s Sartre and Foucault debated the question of the subject in *La Quinzaine Littéraire*.[3] Foucault returned to Sartre's concept of the

[2]In *Existential Marxism in Postwar France* (Princeton: Princeton University Press, 1976), I have described this process as an attempt to supplement Marxism with a theory of the subject.

[3]The responses and counterresponses are found in *La Quinzaine Littéraire* 5 (May 16, 1966), 14; 14 (October 15–31, 1966), 4; 46 (March 1, 1968), 20.

self in an interview with Gérard Raulet, where he applauded the Nietzschean quality of an early essay by Sartre published in a high school journal in 1925, "The History of the Truth."[4] The best discussion by Foucault of the difference between Sartre's concept of the self and his own came in an interview in 1983. He agreed that in many ways his and Sartre's ideas have common parentage in Nietzsche's notion that the self is not given or fixed but created by each individual. Foucault locates in Sartre's concept of authenticity, however, traces of a fixed self, a center, a core: "Through the moral notion of authenticity he turns back to the idea that we have to be ourselves—to be truly our true self." Because we have no "true self," Foucault asserts, "we have to create ourselves as works of art."[5] Sartre looks for the quality of authenticity or bad faith in the relation a person has with him- or herself; Foucault wants to study the discursive practices by which the self establishes the "truth" of itself in the relation it has with itself.

Foucault is right to object to the omniscient voices, universalizing postures, absolute grounds that are strewn throughout Sartre's texts. But he ignores aspects of Sartre's writing that go in the other direction, toward undoing the universal subject. First, Sartre's philosophical texts introduce scenes from daily life: Pierre the waiter, the woman on a date, and the man at the keyhole in *Being and Nothingness*; reading a newspaper, waiting for a bus, and participating in the French Revolution of 1789 in *Critique of Dialectical Reason*. At one level these are merely examples serving philosophical points; at another they are Sartre's philosophy. The little dramas ubiquitously incorporated into the philosophical text obtrude the contingency of daily life into the voice of reason, the absolute epistemological subject. Their presence signifies the failure of reason's self-sufficiency, the dead end of presuppositionless thought. The fiction of Pierre the waiter makes the truth of self-creation just a bit less than universal.

Perhaps more significant, Sartre undermines the universality of his claims in *Critique of Dialectical Reason* by presenting a phenomenology of the discursive subject that resonates in Foucault's Position 3. Sartre here argues that the author *must* totalize the field and *must* do so from a situated position.[6] The author addresses the universal precisely

[4]Gérard Raulet, "Structuralism and Post-structuralism: An Interview with Michel Foucault," trans. Jeremy Harding, *Telos* 55 (Spring 1983), 204.

[5]"How We Behave," interview with Michel Foucault in *Vanity Fair* (November 1983), 65.

[6]Jean-Paul Sartre, *Critique of Dialectical Reason*, vol. 1: *Theory of Practical Ensembles*, trans. Alan Sheridan-Smith (London: New Left Books, 1976), p. 45.

because he or she is a situated subject. Only in the finitude of a place does a perspective on the totality emerge. Looking out from a balcony while on vacation, the (bourgeois) intellectual perceives two workmen on either side of a wall oblivious to each other. The intellectual's view unifies or totalizes the field, introducing a meaning to the entire scene where otherwise there would be none.[7] This totalization of the field, however, is not the only one possible: from another balcony opening onto the same street scene, Simone de Beauvoir might retotalize the field. Perceiving Sartre observing the workmen, she might intervene with a new meaning, one that notes the unity in difference of men, the commonality of Sartre and the workmen, and the relative privilege of all in comparison with women. Behind her, a black servant, having visual access to the street, Sartre, and de Beauvoir, might retotalize the field again, this time introducing a meaning about the unity in difference of whites, be they workmen, intellectuals, or women. Like Mikhail Bakhtin's notion of the dialogic, Sartre's insistence on totalization gives priority to the infinite polysemy of self-creation.

Even granting Sartre these fissures in the rampart of universalism, Foucault's case can still be made. Sartrean self-creation remains rooted in the Western philosophical tradition or, more narrowly, the Enlightenment tradition by its persistent quest for the unity of intelligibility. Sartre struggles in *Critique of Dialectical Reason* not to underscore the antiuniversalist limits of reason but to locate a spot of ultimate totalization, a place from which the situated perspective of the intellectual is harmonious with the collective destiny of mankind. He attempts to locate it in an extended analysis of the Russian Revolution of 1917, in which the conditions for the possibility of dialectical reason are attached to the spiraling totalizations of the class struggle. Sartre tightly grasps the straw of the proletariat as the group subject that contains the potential to create a meaning for mankind, one that self-consciously recognizes the historicity of the freedom of self-creation but nonetheless truly totalizes human experience. The pathos of Sartre's text is the impossibility of this totalization and the equal impossibility of giving it up. For on the other side of this totalization lies the frightening nothingness that the philosophical subject is not transcendent but rooted in power, that dialectical reason is not a condition for the possibility of human freedom.

The issue of universality goes back beyond Hegel to the Enlightenment definition of reason. For Foucault the transition from Position 2 to Position 3 was effected by a reexamination of the Enlightenment. In the important essay "What Is Enlightenment?" Foucault made a final effort to redefine the limits of reason in relation to the question of self-constitution. So important did he consider the interpretation of the Enlightenment that he urged the formation of groups to study it. He defined modern thought as the effort to answer the question "what is enlightenment?"[8] Whereas Positions 1 and 2 presented strong critiques of the Enlightenment, Foucault now reversed himself. There was for him something in the Enlightenment which the methods of archaeology and genealogy did not confront, some "attitude" of the Enlightenment which had to be preserved. This attitude concerned the nature of the subject. Foucault's formulation is worth repeating:

I have been seeking, on the one hand, to emphasize the extent to which a type of philosophical interrogation—one that simultaneously problematizes man's relation to the present, man's historical mode of being, and the constitution of the self as an autonomous subject—is rooted in the Enlightenment. On the other hand, I have been seeking to stress that the thread that may connect us with the Enlightenment is not faithfulness to doctrinal elements, but rather the permanent reactivation of an attitude—that is, of a philosophical ethos that could be described as a permanent critique of our historical era.[9]

This passage needs to be examined carefully because it contains the core of Foucault's Position 3.

The passage concerns an "ethos," a personal position to which Foucault is committing himself in sharp contrast to his authorial stance in Positions 1 and 2. What characterizes Foucault's authorial voice in earlier books is flight. Until the 1980s Foucault's authorial stance shifted, feinted, maneuvered in and around his own pages so as to avoid being fixed by the reader's gaze and by the panoptical stare of the public. During the period of Position 1, Foucault's authorial flight was associated with the structuralist attack on phenomenology: a text was to be read, the structuralists argued, not as a sum of the author's intentions but as the play of signifiers operating at the textual level. Of course this formulation positioned the voice of structuralist authors in an epistemological nowhere, like a hidden god absent from the world of the book. Foucault took a similar position, but to be consistent, he

---

[8]Michel Foucault, "What Is Enlightenment?" trans. Catherine Porter, in Paul Rabinow, ed., *The Foucault Reader* (New York: Pantheon, 1984), p. 32. This essay was presented as a lecture at Berkeley in 1984.

[9]Ibid., p. 42.

refused even to group himself with the structuralists.[10] To do so would define his voice too clearly.

During the 1970s, the phase of Position 2, Foucault's authorial voice did not change, but his reasons for so positioning himself did. At stake now was not so much the antiphenomenological stance but the dynamics of politics. In *The Archaeology of Knowledge* he anticipates the annoyance the reader has with his absence:

Are you going to change yet again, shift your position according to the questions that are put to you, and say that the objections are not really directed at the place from which you are speaking? Are you going to declare yet again that you have never been what you have been reproached with being? Are you already preparing the way out that will enable you in your next book to spring up somewhere else and declare as you're now doing: no, no, I'm not where you are lying in wait for me, but over here, laughing at you?

Foucault responds to the imaginary irked reader with the passage quoted in Chapter 2:

What, do you imagine that I would take so much trouble and so much pleasure in writing, do you think that I would keep so persistently to my task, if I were not preparing—with a rather shaky hand—a labyrinth into which I can venture, in which I can move my discourse, opening up underground passages, forcing it to go far from itself, finding overhangs that reduce and deform its itinerary, in which I can lose myself and appear at last to eyes that I will never have to meet again. I am no doubt not the only one *who writes in order to have no face. Do not ask who I am and do not ask me to remain the same: leave it to our bureaucrats and our police to see that our papers are in order.*[11]

In this extraordinary passage Foucault sees himself as Slothrop in the paranoid vision of Thomas Pynchon's *Gravity's Rainbow*. In the bizarre politics of the twentieth century, invisible forces are at work everywhere, controlling everything. The function of defining the self of the author is therefore repressive; to define the individual is to make him or her into a case, to control in order to study, to objectify for scientific ends. These are the normalizing functions associated with technologies of power, power that is everywhere in society, not merely confined to the state.

[10]See "What Is an Author?" in Donald Bouchard, ed., *Language, Counter-Memory, Practice: Selected Essays and Interviews*, trans. Donald Bouchard and Sherry Simon (Ithaca: Cornell University Press, 1977), pp. 113–38.
[11]Michel Foucault, *The Archaeology of Knowledge and the Discourse on Language*, trans. A. M. Sheridan Smith (New York: Pantheon, 1972), p. 17, my emphasis.

As he moved into Position 3, Foucault realized that authorial absence, while justified on epistemological or political grounds, was damaging to the self of the author and therefore was ultimately inadequate both politically and epistemologically. Foucault had long been concerned with the question of maturity. He typically attacked the positions of others for lack of maturity. In *The Archaeology* again he denounced conventional historians as those who "refuse to grow up,"[12] limiting themselves to discovering filiations in texts rather than probing to deeper archaeological layers. Maturity became a major preoccupation of Position 3 in "What Is Enlightenment?"[13] The mature self was now defined as one with an enlightened attitude, with an ethos of autonomy. Having traced Foucault's positions on the author and on maturity, we may now confront the passage I quoted from "What Is Enlightenment?"

The Enlightenment offers contemporary thinkers no doctrines, no formulated ideas: today these are for the most part elements of liberal ideology. Instead, it presents a historically unique standpoint in which the development of the individual self is associated with a confrontation with the present. The individual recognizes that personal identity cannot be separated from the fate of humanity, and this fate is understood as historically constituted. In this sense maturity designates the insight of the individual's connectedness with the world. On that basis and on that basis alone, Foucault argues, the self may be constituted as autonomous. Maturity means understanding that we cannot escape our heritage from the Enlightenment: "We must try to proceed with the analysis of ourselves as beings who are historically determined, to a certain extent, by the Enlightenment."[14] Foucault was now willing to swallow a bitter pill in order to grow up: his identity as author in flight had to be rejected. The man who defined himself against the Enlightenment, against "reason," against humanism, against "man," who defined himself, therefore, in decentered flight from authorial presence, from the stable ego, the solid subject standing firmly behind his texts, this man now reversed himself once more, only this time in order to accept the parentage of the philosophes.

The philosopher who accepts this status as child of the Enlightenment thereby attains maturity and on that basis lays the foundation for

---

[12]Ibid., p. 144.
[13]See Hubert Dreyfus and Paul Rabinow, "What Is Maturity?" in David Hoy, ed., *Foucault: A Critical Reader* (New York: Blackwell, 1986), pp. 109–22.
[14]Foucault, "What Is Enlightenment?" p. 43.

a critical attitude. The new ethos, manifesting a reconciliation with one's intellectual family, also insists on finitude, on facing self-constitution and the social critique of the present as preeminently historical problems. Foucault writes, "Criticism is no longer going to be practiced in the search for formal structures with universal value, but rather as a historical investigation into the events that have led us to constitute ourselves and to recognize ourselves as subjects of what we are doing."[15] Accepting his own finitude, his own historicity, his own debt to the Enlightenment, Foucault proposes that the philosopher, commit him- or herself and take responsibility for that commitment. The subject becomes an active agent, a point of intelligibility, a self that constitutes itself in relation to history. At this point we may ask if Foucault is merely returning to the positions of Sartre or even Habermas.

The place of the subject in the history of social theory may be outlined in part as follows: liberalism treats the subject as an autonomous, rational, often presocial individual, wary of its rights in relation to other individuals; Marxism treats the subject as a collective agent in contest with other collective agents. In both cases the subject is the ground of history. By the late twentieth century both positions have become unconvincing. Liberalism's subject as citizen and entrepreneur and Marxism's subject as revolutionary proletariat no longer work as characters in the play of human time. In Germany, Adorno and other intellectuals of the Frankfurt School, acknowledging the bleak situation, retreated to the defense of critical theory.[16] In France structuralists such as Althusser theorized history without agents. From the 1970s there has been, in both countries, an effort to reconstruct a theory of the subject as agent of change.

In Germany this effort has centered on the work of Jürgen Habermas. His intricate, encompassing social systematics preserves critique by resurrecting the Enlightenment subject as the autonomous individual. Habermas's subject differs from Marxism by privileging communications over labor. In the massive *Theory of Communicative Action*, Habermas deduces the social conditions for free public speech and regards them as the precondition of democracy.[17] If the conditions of "the ideal speech situation" are fulfilled, the subject emerges as a

[15]Ibid., pp. 45–46.
[16]Theodor Adorno, *Negative Dialectics*, trans. E. B. Ashton (New York: Seabury, 1973).
[17]Jürgen Habermas, *The Theory of Communicative Action*, vol. 1: *Reason and the Rationalization of Society*, trans. Thomas McCarthy (Boston: Beacon, 1984).

rational agent within the intersubjective realm of speech acts. Habermas's subject is also not quite the Enlightenment subject in another sense: in a Hegelian turn, Habermas historicizes the individual in terms of moral development. He relies on the theory of cognitive development of Jean Piaget and Lawrence Kohlberg to support the claim that the human race has evolved to a point where moral maturity is possible.[18] If, in addition, the conditions of public speech are altered to support the "universal pragmatics" of language, freedom will be realized.

From this standpoint Habermas has been appalled by French poststructuralism. In essay after essay he has attacked Foucault, Derrida, Lyotard, and all the defenders of "postmodernity" on the ground that they abandon the Enlightenment and fall into irrationalism and reactionary politics. When the French took positions against rationalism which appeared identical with the pessimism of Adorno and Horkheimer in *Dialectic of Enlightenment*, Habermas was careful to distinguish between Adorno and Horkheimer's antiscientism, which was "recuperable," from the pessimism of the French, which was not.[19] Becoming more and more agitated by the growing influence of the French postmodern thesis, Habermas devoted an entire book to the topic.[20]

But does the Foucault of Position 3 deserve this criticism? Habermas was apparently unaware of any change in Foucault's theory of the self until after the latter's death. In a short piece devoted to "What Is Enlightenment?" Habermas was taken aback by Foucault's reevaluation of the Enlightenment: "Up to now, Foucault traced [the] will-to-knowledge in modern power-formations, only to denounce it. Now, however, he presents it in a completely different light, as the critical impulse worthy of preservation and in need of renewal. This connects his own thinking to the beginnings of modernity."[21] Foucault had changed sides, going over to the camp of modernity against the camp of postmodernity. Habermas interprets the change as Foucault's ad-

[18]Jürgen Habermas, *Communication and the Evolution of Society*, trans. Thomas McCarthy (Boston: Beacon, 1979), pp. 69–94.

[19]Jürgen Habermas, "Modernity versus Postmodernity," *New German Critique*, 22 (Winter 1981), 3–18; and "The Entwinement of Myth and Enlightenment," *New German Critique* 26 (Spring/Summer 1982), 13–30.

[20]Jürgen Habermas, *Der philosophische Diskurs der Moderne: Zwölf Vorlesungen* (Frankfurt: Suhrkamp, 1985).

[21]Jürgen Habermas, "Taking Aim at the Heart of the Present," in David Hoy, ed., *Foucault: A Critical Reader* (New York: Blackwell, 1986), p. 107.

mission of the failure of all his previous work, which betrayed a contradictory effort to base a critique of power on a critique of "truth." Habermas concludes, "Perhaps the force of this contradiction caught up with Foucault in this last of his texts, drawing him again into the circle of the philosophical discourse of modernity which he thought he could explode."[22]

Habermas comes to this conclusion only by eliding the difference between his own concept of the subject and Foucault's. Habermas conserves, as Foucault does not, the Enlightenment concept of the rational subject both as the field of history and as the epistemological point of theory. Foucault, as theoretical subject, confronts the present as difference from and rupture with the past. Habermas, as theoretical subject, transcends the present in a totalization of the past. Habermas derives the individual from the vantage point of the truth value of his historical totalization; Foucault, on the contrary, urges an attitude that claims no truth value for itself but nonetheless an attitude through which the theorist constitutes him- or herself in the present. The difference between the two is crucial. Habermas reconstitutes the Enlightenment subject, the rational, autonomous individual; Foucault constitutes himself as discursive subject by coming to terms with his historical situation.

The status of theory is very different in the two positions. For Habermas, theory is grounded in the truth of a totalization: because of the current position of mankind, the theorist may define truth/ rationality as the ideal speech situation. All other positions may be denounced as reactionary or irrational. For Foucault, self-constitution is established as a relative position against the dominance of scientific discourses/practices that claim to ground themselves in the truth. Not only is the status of theory at odds between the two thinkers. They also differ over the nature of the social field. For Habermas the social is, among other things, the arena for the emergence of rationality; for Foucault it is a multiplicity of technologies of power, which claim rationality for themselves but which are to be opposed on the basis of a self-constitution that seeks "to give new impetus . . . to the undefined work of freedom."[23]

Another way to define Foucault's late position on the subject is to raise the question of universality. The danger of the return to the

---

[22]Ibid., p. 108.
[23]Foucault, "What Is Enlightenment," p. 46.

Enlightenment is the danger of ethnocentrism. The enlightened philosophes in the eighteenth century (and Habermas today) universalize their position. The European intellectual, having discovered reason, speaks for mankind. It bears remembering that the sense of innocence with which the philosophes read the "self-evident" truths of reason was, regardless of their intentions, concurrent with and inevitably an aid, though by no means the only one, to the brutal spread of European power throughout the world. Today that power has been transferred both east and west to the elephantine children of European culture, while Europeans may now more readily accept the relativity of their intellectual products. The issue, then, is how the activity of self-constitution through rational critique of the present can avoid giving universal status to the subject.

After World War II, Sartre recognized the limits of the disengaged intellectual, maturing to a position of commitment. Like the Foucault of Position 3, Sartre saw the necessary relation between self-constitution and political engagement. The existentialist, however, did not hesitate to universalize. In *What Is Literature?* he spoke of commitment: "Every day we must take sides: in our life as a writer, in our articles, in our books." The result was a literature that "manifests the totality of the human condition as a free product of a creative activity."[24] The constitution of the situated, engaged self of the writer authorizes a universal voice. The closer the intellectual approached the conditioned finitude of politics, the more transcendent the constituted subject became. Sartre's argument was novel in its day only because the "universal" values of scientific truth and literary beauty had been associated in bourgeois ideology with ahistorical transcendence. Sartre reversed the poles: engagement was now the path to universality.

Some commentators contend that Foucault is largely successful in avoiding universalist arrogance as well as its relativist opposite because he advocates cosmopolitanism as the attribute of the engaged ethos.[25] Foucault treats the issue in terms of the "generality" of the discourse that emerges from engaged self-constitution. The questions posed by the philosopher are not, he assures us, based on a total, systematic grasp of the present conjuncture. Against Sartre, who ar-

---

[24]Jean-Paul Sartre, *What Is Literature?* trans. Bernard Frechtman (New York: Washington Square Press, 1966), p. 192.
[25]Dreyfus and Rabinow, "What Is Maturity?"

gued that the philosopher must totalize the present in developing his or her problematic, Foucault insists on its particularity. Topics such as insanity, labor, and prisons derive their exigency from the power they impose in the present on the constituting self. The only guarantee invoked by Foucault that these topics have importance beyond the individual's singular preoccupations is "that they have continued to recur up to our time."[26] The mere persistence of the themes, a watered-down version of Nietzsche's eternal return of the same, enhances them with "generality." Generality, for Foucault, derives not from the force of the issue in the present but from its historical repetition.

Foucault errs seriously in this discursive move. By relying on the past to avoid solipsism his position loses its grounding in the present and therefore its potential as a political intervention against dominant discourses. In this respect, Sartre's totalizing position is more to the point. Critical discourses on prisons, sexuality, and so forth contribute to the undoing of particular structures of domination not because of the historical generality of the issue but because these structures can today be judged prevalent and oppressive, a judgment that may, of course, be contested. Foucault's cosmopolitanism unnecessarily retreats from engagement at the crucial moment. He shies away from decisively connecting his late concerns with sexuality and the welfare state with the force of these problematics in the present. Foucault's writing on sexuality appeals to others not because the issue has been raised before but because, without aspiring to the status of a totalization, it nonetheless has weight today.

Another problem in Foucault's return to the Enlightenment concerns the vagueness of the term *self-constitution*. In *Being and Nothingness* Sartre spoke of self-creation as the process of consciousness in which values or meanings are inserted into the world. The ego or self is the sum of projects, of foisting meanings upon nothingness. Sartre qualified the process of self-creation with categories of the situation, being-for-others, being-with-others, and so forth, in an effort to avoid solipsism. Yet the radical freedom of the self to make itself mitigated the force of these alterities. In *Critique of Dialectical Reason* Sartre moved closer to a balanced relation of self and world, but the self remained centered in evanescent consciousness. When Foucault returned to the problematic of the subject in Position 3 he relied on the theme of language rather than consciousness.

---

[26]Foucault, "What Is Enlightenment?" p. 49.

Foucault introduces the problem of self-constitution in *The Use of Pleasure*, volume 2 of *The History of Sexuality*. In the eight years that separated volume 1 from volume 2, Foucault had shifted emphasis: from a concern with the power effects of discursive practices he moved on to look at how the subject responds to them. In his first use of the term *self-constitution*, Foucault writes:

It seemed appropriate to look for the forms and modalities of the relation to self by which the individual constitutes and recognizes himself *qua* subject. After first studying the games of truth in their interplay with one another, as exemplified by certain empirical sciences in the seventeenth and eighteenth centuries, and then studying their interaction with power relations, as exemplified by punitive practices—I felt obliged to study the games of truth in the relationship of self with self and the forming of oneself as a subject.[27]

The question of the subject makes its appearance as a continuation of earlier work rather than as a break with it. Foucault returns to a prestructuralist problematic from the position of a poststructuralist. How successful is this self-described continuity?

If Sartre understood self-constitution as the inner experience of consciousness, Foucault attempts to grasp it as part of the play of social codes, normative discourses, systems of knowledge. One can only applaud Foucault's courage in facing such a difficult task, what he called "a hermeneutics of the self." And one is saddened by knowing that we will never have the fruits of his insight on this question beyond what he has already given us, that is, up to the end of the Hellenistic period.[28] Just as frustrating to me is Foucault's refusal to relate his project to the present. His discussion in the opening pages of *The Uses of Pleasure* concerns the nature of the shift from Position 2 to Position 3, asking the reader's pardon for the delay of publication that necessarily ensued. The reasons he gives for the change concern the importance of the question being posed, not its specific problematization in the present. One could well ask if the question of self-constitution does not in fact derive its urgency and force from its problematization in the present and if that in turn is what raises the issue of its historical transformations.

---

[27]Foucault, *The Use of Pleasure*, trans. Robert Hurley (New York: Vintage, 1985; French edition 1984), p. 6.

[28]Vol. 4 of *The History of Sexuality*, to be titled "Les aveux de la chair" ["The confessions of the flesh"], on the early Christian period, may appear at some time, though Foucault left it incomplete.

Foucault sets the issue of self-constitution in the context of morality. He identifies three types of moral "self-activity": codes of behavior, forms of subjectivation or "forming oneself as an ethical subject," and last, the heart of the issue, self-constitution. To use his words, "A history of the way in which individuals are urged to constitute themselves as subjects of moral conduct would be concerned with the models proposed for setting up and developing relationships with the self, for self-reflection, self-knowledge, self-examination, for the decipherment of the self by oneself, for the transformations that one seeks to accomplish with oneself as object."[29] The first two types of moral self-activity are of less importance to Foucault because, he contends, they did not change drastically in the course of Western history. Moral codes and their imposition on individuals are not the main problem. The third type, self-constitution, on the contrary, is the area of significant change.

For the purposes of this chapter the changes Foucault traces in volumes 2 and 3 are of less interest than is the category of self-constitution. When and how do individuals constitute themselves? Foucault names among his examples of self-constitution Greek discourses on the art of living, the Christian confessional, and the psychoanalytic therapy session. One may ask, however, when one is *not* in a situation of self-constitution. At any moment of daily life the individual may regard him- or herself as an object of moral judgment such that his or her ethical being is in question. The only criterion Foucault would seem to have established for self-constitution is that there exist elaborated and systematized social codes, continuous practices, enduring conventions, and that these serve to demarcate moral questions. But there are a multiplicity of these "institutions" in every society, not only one context—for instance, therapy sessions—in which the events of self-constitution occur.

Foucault isolates sex as the nub of the question without, however, giving much attention to that selection. Western culture, he believes, prescribes the moral "truth" of the individual in his or her sexuality. But are there not business and military codes that may equally serve as the center of the discussion? Are not the entrepreneur and the worker enmeshed in codes and practices in which they constitute themselves as subjects in terms of morals or values?

Could it be said that Foucault selected sexual activity as the venue of

---

[29]Foucault, *The Use of Pleasure*, p. 29.

self-constitution because for him, a gay person, it was a center of his own self-constituting action? Indeed, does not the emergence in the 1970s and 1980s of political movements and subcultures that question traditional forms of self-constitution through sex—the women's movement, the gay and lesbian movements—form the "generality" of Foucault's inquiry? I raise the question not for *ad hominem* reasons but because the issue of the present troubles Foucault's position on the self. While the selection of sex as the arena of self-constitution may be justified on grounds of both historical and present-day importance, it cannot serve to rule out other topics, and it does not successfully delimit the question of self-constitution.

In relation to the present situation, perhaps more important than the issue of sex is that of self-constitution. I contend that self-constitution is undergoing radical changes in the late twentieth century and that Foucault's interpretive genius is manifested in raising that issue. From the perspective of the dominant groups, that is to say, men in elite positions, capitalist culture attempts to confine self-constitution as much as possible to the activity of work. Hence the rise of sexual countermoralities appears to threaten that culture. But I want to focus not on the distinction between the work ethic and the culture of consumption but on another aspect of the category of self-constitution, one that opens up different topics for attention.

This other aspect is language. Foucault in the theme of self-constitution gives greater prominence to language and in a more heuristic manner than other social theorists. The arts of living, the confessional, and the therapy session do not simply privilege sex: they are all *discursive* practices. The individual wrestles with self-constitution through the manipulation of symbols, through carefully elaborated and systematized rules of formation, enunciative statements, and so forth. Military and industrial practices also included codes, but soldiery is proven in battle and work is judged by economic performance. In both cases, action rather than discourse is crucial. As I see it late twentieth-century culture is distinct in that (1) it gives prominence to language and (2) it enacts drastic changes in the structure of language. In what I call the mode of information, everyday life is pervaded by new, electronically mediated language experiences in which the individual is structured to constitute the self and to do so in drastically new ways.

Electronically mediated language structures self-constitution in a double sense. The individual must constitute him- or herself as a consumer; in this way, the mode of information strengthens the hegemonic forces. But the individual must also play with the very process of self-constitution; in this respect, the mode of information undermines the cultural basis of dominant structures. The constitution of self as consumer deserves much attention: the individual continually tests his or her worth against images of the good or the desirable. But the other sense of self-constitution in the mode of information is equally salient. Watching television (especially ads), being monitored by computerized data bases, participating in computer conferencing, or even using computers—all these experiences enact asynchronous discursive practices that heighten the self-referentiality of language and undermine the earlier stability of the subject, the sense of having a continuous identity rooted in time, in space, and in relations with others and things. These discursive practices upset the stability of ego continuity. The anonymity of high-tech "conversations" elicits a play of multiple self-identifications.

The mode of information is the "generality" of Foucault's problematic of self-constitution, or at least it is one possible "generality." Electronically mediated languages constitute a new social region distinct from but overlapping with the capitalist economy, the welfare state, and the nuclear family. Structurally distinct from face-to-face interactions and from printed communications, they emerge into technically advanced societies, undermining the boundary between public and private space. Enlightened and unenlightened subjects alike must take them into account. In a new way they define the self as a locus of truth. Data banks designate the truth of the individual as credit risk, as political subversive, as criminal, as customer, client, agent, friend, parent, and lover. Television advertisements shape the truth of the individual as consumer/commodity, as one whose personality is Calvin Klein, who is the classiness of Members Only jackets or the sleekness of a Camaro, the compassion and caring of one who uses AT&T to "reach out and touch someone." In these and so many other ways, the subject becomes his or her own object of knowledge through electronically mediated exchanges.

If Weber is right that bureaucracies are iron cages of oppression, if Marx is right that capitalism alienates and exploits creative energies, if Freud is right that the nuclear family twists libido into neurosis, then we need also to account for the discursive effects on the subject who constitutes him- or herself in the mode of information.[30]

---

[30]I am preparing an extensive analysis of this problem in *The Mode of Information* (New York: Blackwell, forthcoming).

4

Foucault, the Present, and History

Foucault's historical work initiates a thematic of discontinuity.[1] That much is well known. What is less well recognized is that his work also implies a discontinuity in the present social formation, a discontinuity that resituates the historian's relation to the past, suggests a theoretical reorientation of the historical discipline, and calls for a reexamination of the appropriate topics of historical investigation. Foucault's work enacts this second type of discontinuity without fully recognizing and conceptualizing its contours and significance.

The topics Foucault investigated exemplify a restructuring of historical priorities. Insanity, language, medicine, punishment, sexuality— these have been marginal topics for historians. By placing them at the center of the historical stage Foucault reversed the fundamental theoretical assumptions of the discipline, a reversal that derives its power not only from the strength of Foucault's texts but also from a large-scale social transformation of the second half of the twentieth century, which has led to the mode of information. This chapter explores this theme and assesses its value for the historical discipline.

One's estimate of the significance of Foucault's writings for history depends in every way on which of Foucault's texts one takes to repre-

---

[1]The theme of discontinuity is not set in binary opposition to continuity by Foucault. In works such as *Discipline and Punish* and *The History of Sexuality*, Foucault traces elements of continuity and evolution as well as their opposite. The point is to avoid a totalizing continuity like Hegel's or that which may be found in Whig histories, because they legitimize the present as the culmination of the past.

sent his position. It is possible of course to discover a fundamental unity in his writings. That strategy gives a central role to the author, a position that Foucault himself rejected. A more fruitful interpretation begins with the recognition of a diversity of themes and strategies in his texts, a diversity that is suggested by the marked differences in the recent spate of studies of his works which have appeared in English in recent years. These many books present sharply contrasting interpretations of the nature and significance of his work.[2]

My interest in Foucault derives from my sense that Marxism no longer provides a basis for critical social theory. I have become increasingly troubled by the inability of historical materialism to present an adequate account of the structures of domination in modern society and therefore by its deficiencies as a guide to the social critic and historian. Yet critiques of Marxism often run aground because (1) they fail to specify with appropriate complexity a historical field (usually the political) that cannot be accounted for by the theory of the mode of production and (2) they are unable to provide an epistemological position that would acknowledge the viability of Marxist analyses within a regional domain. In my view *Discipline and Punish* and associated writings by Foucault from the 1970s go a long way toward overcoming the customary limitations of the critiques of historical materialism on both these counts.

The great achievement of *Discipline and Punish* is to theorize and historically analyze a structure of domination in modern society which is beyond the field of investigation opened by the traditional Marxist notion of the mode of production. After *Discipline and Punish* it is no longer possible for Marxist historians to maintain that they alone are able to present a critique of liberal institutions capable of revealing both their structures of domination and their historical specificity. Foucault's history of prisons undermines the liberal view that prisons constituted a humane advance over earlier systems of punishment

---

[2]See, for example, Charles Lemert and Garth Gillan, *Michel Foucault: Social Theory as Transgression* (New York: Columbia University Press, 1982); Pamela Major-Poetzl, *Michel Foucault's Archaeology of Western Culture* (Chapel Hill: University of North Carolina Press, 1983); Hubert Dreyfus and Paul Rabinow, *Michel Foucault: Beyond Structuralism and Hermeneutics* (Chicago: University of Chicago Press, 1982); Barry Smart, *Foucault, Marxism, and Critique* (London: Routledge and Kegan Paul, 1983); John Rajchman, *Michel Foucault: The Freedom of Philosophy* (New York: Columbia University Press, 1985); Mark Cousins and Althar Hussain, *Michel Foucault* (New York: St. Martin's Press, 1984); Karlis Racevskis, *Michel Foucault and the Subversion of Intellect* (Ithaca: Cornell University Press, 1983); Mark Poster, *Foucault, Marxism, and History* (New York: Blackwell, 1985).

and the Marxist view that they are no more than a secondary elaboration of the mode of production. *Discipline and Punish* unveils a specific discourse/practice of domination in modern prisons, which Foucault terms a technology of power, a structure of domination that is invisible when modern history is read through the categories of the mode of production.

The panopticon, as Foucault calls the system of domination specific to prisons, cannot be analyzed from the Marxist historical standpoint because the Marxist categories of alienation and exploitation address only those features of domination which concern the act of labor. Other forms of domination are recognized by Marxist discourse only to the extent that they are rooted in the domination of labor. This limitation of Marxist history is not necessarily a fatal deficiency, since it is characteristic of all theoretical perspectives to open up only particular fields for exploration. There may be problems with the manner in which Marxist theory addresses labor practices (such as the theory of the "false consciousness" of workers who fail to recognize their class interests), but these problems can be corrected by revising the theory; they do not undermine its heuristic value.

The more troubling difficulties with historical materialism derive not so much from the particular categories it generates to enable a critique of the capitalist organization of labor but from the way Marxist theory attempts to monopolize the historical field. When Marx proclaims that the sufferings of the working class are universal and when he contends that domains of practice other than that of labor are superstructural, he is totalizing the historical field, improperly excluding other critical perspectives. In short, he flagrantly reduces all domination to the level of labor. By totalizing the historical field, Marxist history introduces a form of domination at the level of theory and works against the very interests of emancipation it claims to promote.

How is it possible that a theorist who formulated the principle that theory is rooted in the social world, situated in the finitude of practice, should go on to cancel this advance in self-reflexiveness and pretend to elevate his position to that of a universal science? Marx maintained at once that his theory was rooted in the standpoint of the working class and that the position derived from that standpoint is universal in character. Marx's failure to sustain the conditioned, particular, and limited character of the knowledge generated by historical materialism is the source of a theoretical slide back into what Derrida terms the logocentrism of the Western philosophical tradition,[3] the theoretical cause of its regression back to claims of certain truth or, put differently, its appropriation of the surplus value of reason. The implications of this regression are vast for critical theory, Marxist historiography, and much of socialist practice.

The emancipatory interests promoted by historical materialism are sustained only with a detotalized theoretical stance such as that proposed by Foucault, a theoretical asceticism that severely restricts the truth claims of texts. There are two constraints of particular importance: (1) that the historian acknowledge his or her political orientation and (2) that the historian's text not claim to exhaust the meaning of the field to be investigated. *Discipline and Punish* exemplifies both of these self-limiting principles, though it does better with the second than the first, and even regarding the second there are points where the text flirts with totalization.

In *Foucault, Marxism, and History* I demonstrated in detail how *Discipline and Punish* detotalizes the historical field in relation to these self-limiting principles. Here, by contrasting Foucault's position with Marx's, I want to pursue my discussion of "What Is Enlightenment?" and then return to a feature of Foucault's work which concerns a restructuring of the historical field in relation to language.

Foucault's short essay is a remarkably dense statement of position. It outlines nothing less than a new critical theory (reluctant as Foucault was to "theorize"), one that attempts to go beyond the limits of such existing positions as that of the Frankfurt School. The return to Kant—and in particular to his "Was ist Aufklärung?"—signals by itself a reexamination of the fundamental premises of critical theory and points specifically to an effort by Foucault to differentiate his stance from that of Jürgen Habermas. Perhaps most surprising of all to followers of recent French theory is Foucault's willingness in "What is Enlightenment?" to argue for the value to contemporary theory of certain Enlightenment strategies of thought.

The return to Kant, and therefore to the Enlightenment, is also associated with the recent work of Jean-François Lyotard.[4] Lyotard, like Foucault, examined one of Kant's "minor" historical essays, in

---

[3]See Jacques Derrida, *Of Grammatology*, trans. Gayatri Spivak (Baltimore: Johns Hopkins University Press, 1976).

[4]See especially Jean-François Lyotard, *Le différend* (Paris: Minuit, 1984).

this case "The Dispute of the Faculties."[5] Lyotard sought a logical basis of support for epistemological multiplicity, for the positive value of nontotalizing argument. Lyotard's terms *phrase* and later *le différend* mark the boundaries between discourses that are unbridgeable by the ambitions of a total theory. While Foucault's project is similar to Lyotard's, it is at once broader in scope and more politically rooted than his. A detailed comparison of the work of Foucault and Lyotard in the 1970s and 1980s would reveal interesting similarities and contrasts.

Foucault is most sensitive in "What Is Enlightenment?" to the problem of rooting his own project in the Enlightenment. He finds something of interest there, but he does not want his work to be associated too intimately with thinkers of the eighteenth century. Too many people, he complains, put things in the black-and-white terms of pro and contra. He sharply attacks these "blackmailers," because they limit discourse to "a simplistic and authoritarian alternative."[6] Foucault's touchiness on this issue derives from something unresolved at the heart of his essay. The point at stake has to do with his strategy of rooting theory in the present in both ethical and political terms, without, however, adequately determining the relation of the present to the past.

Foucault extracts from the Enlightenment, and from Kant in particular, the problematic of the constitution of the self, relating it to Kant's "dare to know." He contends that Kant introduced into philosophy the novelty of connecting the issue of the "public" freedom to know with "a reflection on history and a particular analysis of the specific moment at which he is writing and because of which he is writing" (38). In other words, the ability to constitute oneself as the subject of knowledge is related to one's intervention in the present as well as one's estimate of the relation of the present to the past. In this formulation rests the achievement of Kant which Foucault would emulate. (In light of Foucault's unfortunately interrupted history of the constitution of the self, it is especially important to analyze Kant's formulation of the problem in relation to the history of modernity.) Foucault carefully delimits his debt to Kant to a particular proposition, a proposi-

[5]See Lyotard, "Judicieux dans le differend" ["Judiciousness in dispute; or, Kant after Marx"], in *Le Faculté de jugement* (Paris: Minuit, 1985). He has also taken up this subject in an unpublished paper whose title might be translated "Philosophy of Phrases."

[6]Michel Foucault, "What Is Enlightenment?" trans. Catherine Porter, in Paul Rabinow, ed., *The Foucault Reader* (New York: Pantheon, 1984), p. 43, hereafter cited parenthetically in the text.

tion, moreover, that is not characteristic of Kant's major works. The charge that Foucault had become a Kantian, much less a philosophe, would appear to be remote. Then why all the fuss about "blackmail"?

For one thing, Foucault is somewhat uncomfortable in the philosophe's garb. He had, after all, devoted many of his early works to a critique of humanist rationalism. From *Madness and Civilization* to *The Order of Things*, he participated in an intellectual current that was animated by the rejection of the Enlightenment. In "What Is Enlightenment?" Foucault distinguishes humanism from the Enlightenment—a distinction not everyone would agree to—reserving his criticism for the former. "Humanism . . . can be opposed by the principle of a critique and a permanent creation of ourselves in our autonomy: that is, a principle that is at the heart of the historical consciousness that the Enlightenment has of itself. From this standpoint, I am inclined to see Enlightenment and humanism in a state of tension rather than identity" (44). Such a definition of the Enlightenment, while arguable, is not widely accepted.

Another issue that disrupts an easy appropriation of the Enlightenment by Foucault concerns his relation to Habermas. In works such as *The Theory of Communicative Action*, "Modernity versus Postmodernity," and "The Entwinement of Myth and Enlightenment," Habermas defends the Enlightenment against thinkers like Foucault precisely on the issue of rationalism.[7] The project of an emancipated society, for Habermas, is impossible without the extension of Enlightenment rationality throughout the space of politics and everyday life. In "Modernity versus Postmodernity" he defends modernity, based on the Enlightenment, against postmodernity, which, he claims, leads to conservatism. In "The Entwinement of Myth and Enlightenment" he rejects as superficial any similarity between the critique of the Enlightenment by Derrida and Foucault, on the one hand, and that by Horkheimer and Adorno, on the other, contending that the pessimism of Horkheimer and Adorno is recuperable while that of Foucault and Derrida is not.[8]

An important change occurred in Habermas's position on this issue

[7]Jürgen Habermas, *The Theory of Communicative Action*, vol. 1, trans. Thomas McCarthy (Boston: Beacon, 1984); Habermas, "Modernity versus Postmodernity," *New German Critique* 22 (Winter 1981), 3–18; Habermas, "The Entwinement of Myth and Enlightenment," *New German Critique* 26 (Spring/Summer 1982), 13–30.

[8]See Max Horkheimer and Theodor Adorno, *Dialectic of Enlightenment*, trans. John Cumming (New York: Seabury, 1972).

at least as early as 1976 in the essay "What Is Universal Pragmatics? but was only fully developed with *The Theory of Communicative Action* in 1981. Habermas now recognized that the defense of the Enlightenment would have to be modified: no longer could it be based on reason as an attribute of consciousness. Instead, Enlightenment rationality must be defended by translating it into a linguistic model. Habermas defined rationality as a capacity for speech in a certain linguistic-social setting. This "ideal speech situation" is conceptualized as a stage in human evolution. Humankind, or at least Western society, is now capable of making a project of constituting the "ideal speech situation" and therefore of constructing an emancipated society.[9] The more recent work more fully elaborates the linguistic character of the concept of reason.

One can plausibly read *The Theory of Communicative Action* in a way that suggests Habermas is closer to the positions of Lyotard and Foucault than might at first be apparent. Although communicative rationality presumes a goal of consensus, a goal with which neither Lyotard nor Foucault has much sympathy, it includes a moment of difference as well. The speaker in Habermas's discourse must be able to contest the proposition of another in order for rationality to be effective in a communication. Support for this reading of *The Theory of Communicative Action* comes in a recent interview of Habermas by Perry Anderson. Here Habermas denies that his defense of rationality on the basis of linguistic consensus leads to "a fully transparent society." On the contrary, he claims that consensus is attained "by means of the criticism of validity claims [and] does not conflict therefore with the pluralism of life forms and interests."[10] Habermas's emphasis on criticism in communication puts him close to Lyotard's notion of *le différend* and to Foucault's notion of oppositional self-constitution, even as it is borrowed from Kant. Foucault's notion of "the constitution of the self as an autonomous subject" (42) bears considerable resemblance to Habermas's notion of communicative rationality as a critical speech act. An additional similarity in the thought of Foucault and Habermas is that they both develop their ideas in relation to the project of emancipation.

The crucial divergence in their ideas, however, concerns the prob-

---

[9]This theme was developed as early as *Communication and the Evolution of Society* (Boston: Beacon, 1979). The German texts were published in 1976.

[10]Perry Anderson, "Jürgen Habermas: A Philosophico-Political Profile," *New Left Review* 151 (May–June 1985), 94.

lem of historical framing. Habermas the dialectician sets the notion of communicative rationality within the context of the total evolution of mankind. His is, in short, a teleological position. Foucault the genealogist roots his position in a detotalized confrontation with the present. On the question of historical framing, Habermas retreats to an assumption of epistemological certainty if only in the sense that the critical theorist must be able to reconstruct the entire past. Foucault's position requires a much more modest claim for the critic: that he or she can dare to know and constitute him- or herself in political opposition to present structures of domination. Foucault's position therefore goes further than Habermas's toward abandoning the traditional, essentialist view of the subject as centered in knowledge.

The main theoretical problem at stake in the appropriation of the Enlightenment, however, is the issue of how to change the present. Foucault argues very powerfully for a new kind of criticism, which he calls "a limit attitude." The new criticism seeks to determine what is and what is not possible. Foucault's proposal is, in many ways, closer to Marx's than to Kant's thinking. Kant defined what reason could *not* do, thereby rejecting earlier forms of metaphysical discourse. The powers of rationality which remained after Kant's philosophical housecleaning were determined through the strategy of the transcendental deduction, which rooted pure reason in universality. By contrast, both Marx and Foucault place temporal limits on reason, restricting it by its contingency, its presentness. The limits of reason are determined by the finitude of the thinker, by his or her situation.

In addition both Marx and Foucault, however differently, orient the task of criticism to the "positive" goal of transgression. Foucault was never more clear on this issue than in "What Is Enlightenment?" The project of criticism is associated with the labor of freedom: reason unmasks pretensions to universality, reveals the boundaries of social and cultural forms, and points to the possibility of alternative forms that are not yet associated with domination. Foucault goes considerably beyond Marx in the connection he makes between the transgressive critique of the present and the constitution of the self. Much more clearly than Marx, Foucault insists that historical writing is a form of self-determination as well as a practice of social critique. In Foucault's words, "I mean that this work done at the limits of ourselves must, on the one hand, open up a realm of historical inquiry and, on the other, put itself to the test of reality, of contemporary reality, both to grasp the points where change is possible and desirable, and to determine the precise form this change should take" (46). Marx, in many ways a son of the Enlightenment, never saw that the critique of the present was authorized by the contingency of the constitution of the self of the critic. Instead, in a variation on the theme of essentialist rationalism, Marx presumed the universal validity of the dialectic.

"What Is Enlightenment?" synthesizes two strains in Foucault's work since the early 1970s. *Discipline and Punish* and volume 1 of *The History of Sexuality* present critiques of domination by providing detotalized histories of particular discourses/practices. Subsequently Foucault worked on the problem of the constitution of the self, exploring that theme in volumes 2 and 3 of *The History of Sexuality*. But the connection between these two lines of research were not drawn out until "What Is Enlightenment?" The enigmatic proclamation in *Discipline and Punish* that Foucault's history is a history of the present now becomes clear. Criticism, of which historical writing is one form, begins with the critic's self-constitution, and that occurs through the recognition of one's contingency and, at the same time, the recognition that social domination is contingent. Foucault's formulation is worth repeating: "I shall thus characterize the philosophical ethos appropriate to the critical ontology of ourselves as a historico-practical test of the limits that we may go beyond, and thus as work carried out by ourselves upon ourselves as free beings" (47).

The weak point of Foucault's new history rests with the problem of the generality of the historian's work, a problem Foucault recognizes and addresses but does not completely resolve. The historian's work begins with his or her recognition of contingency and subsequent constitution of self as historian. Thus for Foucault the historian's work is ultimately one of self-examination. With an interior focus having priority over the labor of reconstructing the past, the historian is subject to the blind spot of social determination. Historical writing for him is rooted in the inward investigation of limits; its strategy of outward investigation of social domination may therefore lack systematicity, lack a grasp of the general structures that work to determine the contingency of the individual. Foucault grapples with this problem by outlining what he regards as the "generality" of his problematic: "This philosophical attitude has to be translated into the labor of diverse inquiries . . . [which] have their theoretical coherence in the definition of the historically unique forms in which the generalities of our relations to things, to others, to ourselves, have been problematized" (50). Foucault here maintains that historical writing, however "monographic" or limited in scope, implicates large theoretical issues. These issues ("relations to things, to others, to ourselves") are definitions of general questions. The problem with Foucault's position is that he privileges the historian's relations to others and things in comparison to the historian's relation in him- or herself. Part of the contingent situation of the historian is the world in which he or she attempts the constitution of self. Yet in Foucault's essay there is no attempt to characterize the general patterns of this world or, better, no attempt to determine the particularity of the social world that gives force to the investigations of the historian. What the reader confronts in Foucault's text is a world in which there are diverse forms of domination and diverse forms of resistance to domination. One finds no recognition of a special character of the contingent present that makes pertinent a form of historiography such as the one Foucault develops.

It is my conviction that the new language experiences that have emerged in the recent past, which I call the mode of information, work to detotalize the social world, providing the impetus for a decentered form of historiography such as Foucault's. It is also my conviction that the explicit recognition and analysis of the mode of information provides supplementary force to the main lines of Foucault's work, giving it a power that it otherwise lacks. His position, as it stands, remains subject to the charge that it generates arbitrary projects, that its problematic is unable to argue for the general value and applicability of its conclusions.

The additional force that might be added to Foucault's position by incorporating the perspective of the mode of information can be briefly sketched. The problematic of the constitution of the self in contemporary social space must take account of electronically mediated communications, which are increasingly being substituted for both face-to-face and written communications. Today, television takes over the role of the confessional and the therapy session of earlier times. It presents "discourses" that operate to "constitute the self" of the viewer. Television is a complex phenomenon in which network serials and news, advertisements, and tapes of movies played on video cassette recorders have very different effects on the question of the subject. In the case of advertisements, the viewer is fashioned into a consumer-subject by the visual and aural rhetoric, with floating signifiers attached to commodities not by any intrinsic relation to them but by the logic of unfulfilled desire, which is at once imprinted in the subject's fantasy and already there through the limits of the social order.

In the case of computer mail and teleconferencing temporal and spatial distance continuously structures the subject to constitute him- or herself in the discourse.[11] Electronic mediation heightens the "artificiality" of communication, extending to the ultimate degree the *différance* of writing. In a telephone conversation the receiver of the message may have an illusion of being there with the sender, an illusion of presence, but in the case of electronic mail and teleconferencing no such illusion is supported. Writing appears as anonymous signs on a screen, coming from nowhere or anywhere, occurring immediately or at any time in the past.

Self-constitution is built into the structure of the communication. With the mode of information, the question of the subject is no longer limited to the opposition consciousness/structure. Instead, the subject becomes a multiplicity of self-constitutions, with one identity as the receiver of television ads, another as operator of an automatic teller, another as a reader of novels, and so forth. Foucault's problematic of self-constitution is the appropriate strategy for the mode of information, finding its most extensive field in that context.

Foucault's reluctance to problematize the character of the social world stems no doubt from the failures of the characterization provided by Marxists and the epistemological implications of that failure.[12] But the impasses at all levels of the theory of the mode of production and the dangers of totalization inherent in the project of characterizing the social world are not adequate excuses. A detotalized analysis of the social world, one that defines emergent structures in our social space, remains both possible and necessary. For without such an analysis Foucault remains unable to distinguish the difference in the respective situations of Kant and himself, and therefore remains uneasy in returning to Kant because of the danger that an identity of positions might appear to result. Yet if Foucault had defined his present in its difference from Kant's (postmodern vs. modern; mode of information vs. mode of production) the danger of the confusion of

[11]I am indebted to Andrew Feenberg and Rob Kling for stimulating this line of thought.

[12]That is, that the revolutionary subject and the subject of revolutionary theory cannot be the basis of a project of universal emancipation.

positions would disappear and the return would become a graceful exchange, not subject to "blackmail" of any sort.

It is necessary to theorize, therefore, as one moment in the constitution of the historian's subjectivity and discourse a characterization, however provisional, of the historian's social world. To summarize, the benefits of this endeavor are two: (1) to provide specificity and difference to the historian's situation and (2) to give generality to his or her transgressive investigations. I will now illustrate these themes by comparing Marx to Foucault and indicating how a theory of the mode of information enhances both of their historical perspectives.

Marx constitutes the historical field as one predominantly of action, specifically laboring action. In contrast, Foucault gives priority to discourse, a form of language, without severing the relation of discourse to practice. Foucault carried out this paradigmatic shift in the context of the strong current of structuralism in France. Structuralists not only privilege linguistic phenomena, they tend to reduce the entire field of the human sciences to language. Foucault rejects the structuralist totalization of language with his insistence on the couplet discourse/practice, thereby avoiding the danger of formalism. The problem, however, is that he accepts the paradigm shift toward language without questioning the social factors (such as the mode of information) that give urgency to the move.

Marx shifted the field from politics to labor, arguing not only that labor had not yet been adequately theorized but that the current social formation *drew attention to labor as a problem* in that capitalism transforms the labor process. Foucault shifted the field from labor to discourse *without a rigorous examination* of the ways the contemporary field problematizes language. He partially contextualized the shift to language in that he drew attention to the new role of the human sciences in structures of domination, a Nietzschean theme that he renewed with great success. But he never thoroughly examined the drastic transformations of linguistic experience in the contemporary field. The result is that his texts do not reveal as fully as they might the powerful social forces that justify the emphasis on language as a focus of historical investigation.[13]

---

[13]A similar criticism could be made of Jürgen Habermas. In "Technology and Science as 'Ideology,'" *Toward a Rational Society: Student Protest, Science, and Politics*, trans. Jeremy Shapiro (Boston: Beacon, 1970), he supplements the Marxist concept of labor with the category of symbolic interaction (p. 88). Yet he does so without a discussion of the contextual impulses that somehow authorize the supplement or make it urgent.

I have been developing the concept of the mode of information to accomplish just that purpose. Unlike such terms as the "age of information," the mode of information does not designate a new period of history. Conceptualized in that way, the mode of information would totalize the field, reintroducing the problem that plagues Marx's concept of the mode of production. I employ the concept of the mode of information to designate the field of linguistic experience, whose basic structural relations change from period to period just as do those of the mode of production. But Marx's concept of the mode of production tends to slide in its usage from a stipulation that there are different modes of production at different times to a depiction of the modern epoch (capitalism) as a social system dominated by the forces and relations of production. The simple theoretical observation that all societies include structures through which human beings produce objects to satisfy their needs is transformed into a reductive totalization that centers the historical field in the system of production. This theoretical slippage must be avoided in the development of the concept of the mode of information. This category must not be theorized in such a way that it appears that the current period substitutes a mode of information for a mode of production.

The need to develop a historical field of investigation constituted by the mode of information derives both from the failure of historical materialism (as well as other positions, such as Max Weber's) to elaborate a theory of language and from fundamental changes in linguistic experience which have occurred in the twentieth century. In view of the limitations of this chapter, I will focus only on the second issue. An adequate theory of the mode of information crucially depends upon the way the context of language is envisioned. It is true that the human sciences in the twentieth century have become associated with systems of social control. It is true that the mode of production has been significantly altered in recent years by the introduction of information-processing systems. But neither of these contextual changes is an adequate starting point for developing a concept of the mode of information because neither comes to terms with the general problem of the position of language in social relations, neither, in short, formulates a theory of the relation of language to action.

The theory of the mode of information must take into account the critiques of the representationality, intentionality, and univocality of language which have developed in such variety in recent decades. The structuralists derive meaning not from the consciousness of the language speaker but from the system of binary opposites at a synchronous level of analysis. Semiologists demonstrate that meanings can "float" in social space and be attached to objects in a manner out of phase with their "utility" or referentiality. Deconstructionists argue for the "textuality" of spoken language, the systematic gap between intention and discourse. Speech-act theorists insist on the performative component of utterances, denying that statements are reducible to the function of truth. M. M. Bakhtin uncovers a dialogic dimension of language in which polyvocality and polysemy disrupt the illusion of semantic stability.[14] Each of these positions impressively argues against positivism and formalism.

However valuable these recent and, in many cases, "postrationalist" theories of language may be, they do not offer the historian the principles of structural variation which constitute a linguistic field *at the temporal level*.[15] While many of these positions include suggestive analytic perspectives on the question of context, they do not elaborate its internal complexity and differences. They do not specify the uniqueness of linguistic experience in the present conjuncture. Their categories tend to capture language in a way that presents it as a structurally unchanging phenomenon. What is required for a theory of the mode of information is a set of categories which prepares for the analysis of historical difference.

This large theoretical task cannot be approached in the context of this chapter, but I do want to indicate the kinds of linguistic phenomena which appear to have recently arisen and which require historical analysis. If, beginning in the sixteenth century, the printing press transformed linguistic experience, so in the twentieth century have electronic forms of information storage and transmission. A great body of linguistic interaction now occurs at tremendously expanded distances of space and time. The telephone, radio, television, and the computer—all encourage a dispersal of communicating groups. Al-

---

[14]Perhaps the most interesting text to consult on the structuralist position is Roland Barthes, *The Fashion System*, trans. M. Ward and Richard Howard (New York: Hill and Wang, 1983; 1st ed. 1967). On semiology, see Jean Baudrillard, *The Mirror of Production*, trans. Mark Poster (St. Louis, Mo.: Telos Press, 1975; 1st ed. 1973). On deconstruction, see Derrida, *Of Grammatology*. On speech-act theory, see J. L. Austin, *How to Do Things with Words* (Cambridge: Harvard University Press, 1962). On the dialogic dimension of language, see M. M. Bakhtin, *The Dialogic Imagination*, trans. Michael Holquist (Austin: University of Texas Press, 1981).

[15]For a different opinion, see Dominick LaCapra, *Rethinking Intellectual History* (Ithaca: Cornell University Press, 1983).

though this dispersal began with printing, it is necessary to consider whether so vast an extension of distancing institutes a qualitative transformation of social interaction. I maintain that subjects are constituted differently when a good part of their communicative experience is mediated by electronic discourse/practice. In his last years Foucault worked on the question of the constitution of the subject; his project must be extended to include the mode of information.

One structural feature of the electronic media which differentiates them from printing is their complex multidirectionality. Print sends signifiers out from a source; the computer *collects* signifiers from everywhere. Print extends the "influence" of a communicating subject or text; the computer allows the receiver of signifiers to monitor the transmitter. Centers of power become panoptical addressees whose "memory" is a new structure of domination. One landlord in Los Angeles entered into his computer information about the behavior of his tenants and made that available to other landlords, at a price.[16] Communicational experience has been altered: the electronic media encourage the dispersal of the community but, at the same time, facilitate its surveillance.

The market is also transformed. Semiologists such as Baudrillard have analyzed the structure of signification in advertising, stressing the separation of the signifier and its subsequent recoding of commodities. The electronic media promote this process. Anything can be associated with anything else for a viewing subject who is structured by the rhetoric of the commercial. President Reagan, a media person par excellence, attempted to associate a visit to Nazi SS graves with United States–West German alliance. He was surprised that many groups held on to signifiers about the graves which contradicted the move of reconciliation. What is germane here is not the resistance of communicational communities whose "data storage" read out SS equals murderers but that Reagan reenacted the new structure of the mode of information, in which meanings are manipulated by transmitters. Leisure and labor, too, must be analyzed in terms of the new mode of information.

The relation between the computer and its user requires study. The computer is not written upon like a blank sheet of paper. First, the

[16]See Gary Marx, "The New Surveillance," *Technology Review* (May–June 1985), 43–48.

patterned, lighted pixels on the screen are not like marks of ink or graphite. They are "immaterials,"[17] not inertial traces. The user's mind is confronted not by the resistance of matter but by a screen with a new ontological status: half matter, half idea. The text on a computer screen is as evanescent as a speaker's words, instantaneously available for correction or change. So an individual creates texts in a computer by interacting with an "object" that is more like the writer's brain than like a piece of paper.

Next, the computer can be the brain, that is, it can access data bases that resemble memory but vastly extend some of memory's capabilities. Without any claim about the intelligence of the computer, it is nonetheless able in principle to make available the corpus of the world's texts, thus in practice transforming the user's memory.[18] In addition, the computer can substitute for the speaker in a conversation. Besides regulating machines, it can act communicationally in place of people. The traditional, Cartesian view of the human subject as speaker who acts on the world of nature must be modified to account for these new "agents."

The electronic means of communication explode the space-time limits of messages, permit the surveillance of messages and actions, complete the process of the automation of production, despatialize certain kinds of work, enable signifiers to float in relation to referents, become a substitute for certain forms of social relations, provide a new relation between author and text, infinitely expand human memory, and undermine the Cartesian ontology of subject and object. In these ways "reality" is constituted in the "unreal" dimension of the media. There are no more pure acts, only linguistically transformed representations, which are "acts" themselves. These features of the new mode of information are suggested as a tentative outline, nothing more. Even in this preliminary form they depict a drastically new character of linguistic experience with inestimable significance for the reconstitution of the social world, including entirely new structures of domination. Historians committed to the project of emancipation in its liberal,

---

[17]This term was coined by Jean-François Lyotard for his Beaubourg exhibit in 1985.

[18]While the debates over artificial intelligence (AI) are very important and concern advanced features of the latest computer technology, I prefer to focus on relatively simple technical accomplishments. I believe that AI, with its focus on "intelligence," pays attention to only one aspect of the question of the relation of the subject to the computer.

Marxist, or any other form need to concern themselves with the analysis of the mode of information, a project in which the theory of the mode of production will be of minimal assistance.[19]

[19]Some interesting empirical work on various aspects of the mode of information are Starr Roxanne Hiltz and Murray Turoff, *The Network Nation: Human Communication via Computer* (London: Addison-Wesley, 1978), on computer conferencing; and Marie Marchand, *La grande aventure du Minitel* (Paris: Larousse, 1987), on electronic message services.

5

Foucault and the
Tyranny of Greece

In *Foucault, Marxism, and History*, I argue that Foucault's writings, especially those of the 1970s, offer the most suggestive positions available for the reconstitution of critical theory and history.[1] In *Discipline and Punish* and volume 1 of *The History of Sexuality*, he presents an effective critique of totalizing positions and traditional epistemological strategies. In addition he proposes a new kind of history based on the key concepts of discourse/practice and technologies of power, which go a long way toward overcoming the limitations of critical theory and historical writing. His texts treat the question of language in a manner that bypasses the theoretical obstacles inherent in dualist assumptions about idealism and materialism, thought and action, reason and nature, effectively opening new paths for analysis and critique. These texts also develop a position that reorients critical theory to the particular social context of the mode of information. More than anyone else, Foucault aligns his discursive strategy to the new constraints and systems of domination unique to the late twentieth century. In the present conjuncture a new social formation is emerging in which science is implicated in power; in which the process of production is dependent as never before on discourse and knowledge; in which organized systems of power (bureaucracies) rely upon information gathering, storage, and retrieval; in which communication patterns increasingly consist of electronically mediated interactions. These new

[1]Mark Poster, *Foucault, Marxism, and History* (London: Blackwell, 1984).

features of the social landscape, taken together, are what I call the mode of information. And Foucault's last works, with all their innovations, enable critical theory to analyze its important characteristics and explore the new, multiple mechanisms of domination emerging within it. The question I address in this chapter is whether and how volumes 2 and 3 of *The History of Sexuality* further the advances contained in the texts of the 1970s.

Sex is among the most difficult topics in the human sciences. Sex appears to be primordial, natural, a biological given that resists historical analysis and a critical theoretical perspective. Even diet, which resembles sex in having a strong biological ground, is more amenable to analysis in terms of class differences, cultural patterning, and elaborate social rituals. But sex seems either always the same thing or subject to variations that are of limited hermeneutic interest. Demographic studies treat variations in sexual activity but do so in an objectified analysis that reduces sexual practice to reproduction.[2] Intellectual historians deal only with attitudes toward sex, suggestively relating them to other conceptual patterns but failing to embody the analysis in the important context of social practice.[3] Sex remains for historians of ideas a curious and marginal sector of the mansions of the mind. Freudians do a little better. They interpret sex in relation to personality formation and its vicissitudes in the adult psyche. Yet they are saddled with a notion of a fixed core of desire, an unchanging sediment of unconscious libido, an ontology of sex as a residue of nature in an evolving process of civilization.[4] To appreciate the significance of Foucault's project on the history of sexuality, it is necessary to remind oneself of the limited success this topic has had in the field of the human sciences.

Many readers will be disappointed by volumes 2 and 3. They might argue that these volumes do not sustain the powerful problematic developed in *Discipline and Punish* and volume 1 of *The History of Sexuality*, a problematic that seemed to be the culmination of Foucault's work since *Madness and Civilization*. The analytics of discourse/

---

[2]See, for example, Edward Shorter, "Illegitimacy, Sexual Revolution, and Social Change in Modern Europe," in T. Rabb and R. Rotberg, eds., *The Family in History* (New York: Harper and Row, 1971), pp. 48–83.

[3]See, for example, Paul Robinson, *The Modernization of Sex* (New York: Basic, 1977). An interesting effort that combines intellectual, social, and political history is Jeffrey Weeks, *Sex, Politics, and Society* (London: Longman, 1981).

[4]The best example is Herbert Marcuse, *Eros and Civilization* (Boston: Beacon, 1955).

practice and of technologies of power, which were the theoretical centerpieces of the previous two works, are almost completely gone. His splendid maneuver in volume 1, which bypassed the theory of repression in favor of an analysis of discourses on sex, is now abandoned. So too is the delicate, complex hermeneutic that displaced standard forms of intellectual history with an analysis that successfully revealed the imbrication of discourse in power. Volumes 2 and 3 of *The History of Sexuality*, on the contrary, might appear to those who have enjoyed Foucault's previous work to be an exercise in paraphraxis, a string of banal summaries of well-known texts, a succession of unimaginative readings of the classics by someone who is not very well versed in the field. Ancient historians in both France and the United States greeted the volumes with surprising enthusiasm, though they did complain in an expected way that Foucault chose to discuss such unrepresentative figures as Artemidorus, that he was not familiar enough with the secondary literature, and that he did not set ideas in their social context.[5] Moreover, the magnificent writing of the earlier books, it might be argued, writing that continually surprised and delighted the reader with rhetorical devices and conceptual twists, becomes in the new books flat, straightforward, even unimaginative.

Shortly before he died Foucault gave an interview, subsequently published in *Les Nouvelles*,[6] in which he responded to some of these objections. On the question of style, for example, he retorted that he self-consciously adopted a new voice back in the mid-1970s as a result of adding a new dimension, the individual, to his problematic of truth and power. Not every critic will be convinced by this response. Indeed, many will attribute what they regard as a decline in the new books to an exhaustion of his creative powers. Alternatively, they may complain that the books appeared prematurely, that Foucault unwisely rushed to publication only because he knew he had little time left. Other, even less kind critics will attribute the failings of the books to Foucault's inability to distance himself from a topic that was close to

[5]Historians in France first warmly greeted vols. 2 and 3. Perhaps it seemed to them that Foucault was at last doing "real" history. See Aline Rousselle's review in *Annales: Economies, Sociétés, Civilisations* 42 (March–April 1987), 317–21. Specialists in ancient history and philology in the United States were also generally pleased. See, for example, Vern Bullough's review in the *American Historical Review* 90 (April 1985), 387–88; and David Halperin "Sexual Ethics and Technologies of the Self in Classical Greece," in *American Journal of Philology* 107 (1986), 274–86.

[6]"Le retour de la morale," *Les Nouvelles* (June 28–July 5, 1984), 37–41.

his own homosexuality. These criticisms, while partially valid, fail to address the main issue in *L'usage des plaisirs* and *Le souci de soi*,[7] which is the constitution of the self through discourses on sex, a problematic that would have yielded its full potential, I am convinced, only with the completion of the project in volumes devoted to the modern period.

In volumes 2 and 3 of *The History of Sexuality* there are only fleeting references to Foucault's interpretive strategy of genealogy.[8] This sparsity does not mean that these books reject the older method. On the contrary, Foucault introduces *L'usage des plaisirs* with a methodological discussion that adheres to the tenets of genealogical analysis. He dismisses attempts to write a history of sex as a history of regulative codes or a history of ideas. To the surprise of the reader, he claims that at the level of codes things have not changed all that much. The Greeks and Romans were often like the Christians and the moderns in preferring monogamous, heterosexual, procreative sex. To obtain an adequate grasp of sexual phenomena it is necessary, Foucault contends, to leave the terrain of desire and its repressions and move to a problematic in which sex is understood in relation to the moral level of self-constitution. The important question for him—and it is a brilliant maneuver—is to reverse the normal expectation and ask why and in what ways sex is a problem for the individual in his or her effort to lead a moral life. "In brief, in this genealogy the idea was to investigate how individuals have been led to exercise on themselves, and on others, a hermeneutic of desire in which their sexual behavior has no doubt been the focus, but certainly not the exclusive one" (11). If it is assumed today that sex is central to one's identity, Foucault asks why this is so, why has it been so in the past, and how has its form of being so changed.

The History of Sexuality is genealogical in that it opens up for historical questioning that which we assume to have always been the case. It is also genealogical in the sense that this opening displaces earlier methods of analyzing the problem and attempts to sustain the method of discourse/practice employed in earlier studies. Instead of placing the analysis of texts on sex in the couplet science-ideology, Foucault attempts to look at the way discourses and practices generate an

---

[7]"Les aveux de la chair," the promised vol. 4 of *The History of Sexuality* dealing with the early Christian era, has not appeared on schedule and may be delayed for some time.

[8]*L'usage des plaisirs* (Paris: Gallimard, 1984), p. 11, hereafter cited parenthetically in the text. Translations are my own.

experience of sex. In this regard, Foucault is unable to sustain the level of analysis of his earlier works. There is in his writing here simply too much discourse and not enough practice. His chapters read too much like intellectual histories of different writings on sex with few references to social practice. In this sense these volumes are uncharacteristic of Foucault, and the shortcoming might be due to the paucity of evidence from Greek, Roman and early Christian periods. That question will be decided by those more expert than I in the appropriate fields. The result is that the fine balance so evident in *Discipline and Punish* between the analysis of discourse and the play of practice is too often lost. In the *History of Sexuality* discourse is the only practice.

Foucault is more successful with another aspect of genealogical analysis which is easily overlooked. We might ask why Foucault found it necessary to go back to the Greeks. In his earlier works he never crossed the line that divides the modern world from its antecedents, and in the 1970s his custom was to begin with the eighteenth century. Besides, he is surely taking a risk by going back so far in time to a period with which he cannot be very familiar. Although he does refer to many important primary and secondary works on the ancient period, it is unlikely that he had the mastery of the materials of these epochs that he displayed in works on modernity. There is every reason to examine the cause for his departure from his habitual terrain. The answer lies in the requirements of the method of genealogy.

One of the salient features of Foucault's work has been that he begins at a point of difference. In *Madness and Civilization* it was the ship of fools on which the insane are visibly and drastically excluded from society; in *The Order of Things* it was the episteme of correspondences, through which words and things have an intrinsic relation that today is difficult even to imagine; in *Discipline and Punish* it was the torture system of punishment with the cruel public dismemberment of Damiens the regicide. In each case, he addressed and analyzed a phenomenon that appears strange, discomforting, unfamiliar, vaguely threatening to the modern sensibility. The same procedure is followed in *The History of Sexuality*. The Greeks are the starting point for Foucault because in their sexual practice the love between free, adult males and boys was the central question. What is more, love for boys is not merely a point of difference with regard to sexual desire. It is also different in that sexual desire was not the problem for the Greeks, rather it was individual freedom or ethics.

Foucault begins his *History of Sexuality* with the Greeks because only by going back that far in time can he locate a moment when the question of sex is posed in terms of a different relationship (adult males to boys) than that of the present and when sex is placed in a different register from that of the present (freedom rather than desire). The result of this genealogical strategy is to let us see with fresh eyes our own sexuality in comparison with the point of difference. What must be avoided at all costs is reversing poles of the values at stake. Thus, Foucault does all he can to undermine a nostalgic presentation of Greek sexuality, a problem he finds in the work of others who have trod a similar path to pre-Christian sexual codes.[9] The critical intention of genealogical analysis is to reveal a difference in a phenomenon in such a way that it undermines the self-certainty of the present without presenting the past as an alternative. An underlying drama in the text of *L'usage des plaisirs* is that Foucault wants to present the Greek practice of the love of boys as a point of difference without adding any positive valuation to it, even though he is himself a homosexual and associated with the gay rights movement (although he has expressed reservations about various tendencies within that movement, especially those concerning the ideology of "rights" and "liberation"). To be sure, contemporary homosexuality bears little resemblance to Greek practices, as Foucault underscores. Nonetheless, there are enough superficial similarities to cause concern. Perhaps Foucault overcompensates for the likeness by denying all similarities.

The great achievement of the genealogical analysis of sex rests with its ability to present a critical history that undermines the unquestioned legitimacy of the present by offering a re-creation of a different past. The rupture between the past and the present generates the space for critique. This history avoids both teleology or progressivism and nostalgia. Foucault's history is a form of rationalist asceticism, rigorously denying to the historian all utopian impulses. In *The History of Sexuality* there are no golden ages and no inevitable evolutions toward perfection in the future. Nonetheless, by undermining the assumed universality of the pattern of sexuality in the present, Foucault's genealogy opens up the question of the limitations of sex in the present, implicitly inviting those disadvantaged by it to develop strategies to change it. In this sense Foucault is a historical materialist in the best Marxist sense.

Even more than a Marxist, Foucault, especially in *The History of*

---

[9]See his discussion of this problem in "Le retour de la morale," pp. 39–40.

Sexuality, demonstrates his debt to Nietzsche, in this case on terrain that is close to that of the anchorite of the nineteenth century. In *On the Genealogy of Morals* Nietzsche contrasted the good-bad morality of the master class with the good-evil morality of the slaves.[10] The Greek ruling class was one of the chief examples of the master morality for Nietzsche, who was trained in the classics and in methods of philology. The social position of the master led directly, according to him, to a spontaneous valuation of what was considered good along with a corresponding distaste or negative valuation of what was considered bad. Like Nietzsche, Foucault attributes to this master class a morality of freedom, a sense of unrestrictedness, so foreign to the present morality with its compulsions and its guilt. Even the themes of austerity Greek masters introduced into their morality must be understood, Foucault insists, as an "elaboration and stylization of an activity in the exercise of power and the practice of freedom" (30). In the context of a luxurious, open life situation, the Greek masters, in *L'usage des plaisirs*, determine their individual constraints or, in Foucault's terms, constitute their own selves. Neither Nietzsche nor Foucault idealizes the master morality: Nietzsche saw in the masters uninteresting stupidity; Foucault finds the Greek rulers mired in "a profound error."[11]

Nietzsche and Foucault differ in the accents they give to the Greek master morality. Nietzsche emphasizes the great healthiness (*die grosse Gesundheit*) of the Greeks, the exuberance and power of their morality; Foucault stresses the constraints that, although self-imposed, they wrestled with. The love of boys was the central, nagging moral issue for the Greeks because that practice, Foucault argues, brought into question their style of life. For most writers in the fourth to the second centuries B.C., there were no constraints on sexual passion. Anyone—wife, mistress, slave, boy—could become a love object for a Greek master. To lead a moral life a Greek master need only actively decide on a course of action. This ruling class valued the active posture because it alone was commensurate with their freedom and their freedom alone ensured the health of the polis. With regard to sexual practice, they associated activity with penetration. The moral issue for them concerned the propriety and possible injurious consequences of placing boys from the ruling class in a passive position

---

[10]Friedrich Nietzsche, *On the Genealogy of Morals*, trans. W. Kaufmann (New York: Vintage, 1967).

[11]Foucault, "Le retour de la morale," p. 38.

during sexual relations with free adult males (277). The masters developed an elaborate etiquette, outlined in many discourses, because they feared that the practice of the love of boys might inure the boys to patterns of passivity, hence undermining their freedom and the freedom of the polis. In this way sex became a moral problem in a culture where desire itself was not a moral issue. The love of boys was the leading preoccupation in the elaboration of techniques of the self by which the masters constituted themselves in their freedom.

Foucault outlines several features of these techniques of the self which underscore the difference between Greek and modern forms of sexuality. The codes and restrictions that governed sex were minimal, a sharp contrast with the Christian period, when sexual regulations were detailed and comprehensive. Then too, the Greeks considered sex good, the Christians, bad or evil. Also the Greeks did not place sexual practice in a universalist context; each individual had to determine the pattern of sexual objects and practices—again the opposite of the Christians. Marriage for the Greeks was more a social and political arrangement than a joining of two souls in a sacred relationship as it would later become. Thus for the Greeks there was no preoccupation with the self as a desiring subject, no careful scrutiny of the validity of one's sexual impulses. It followed that the Greeks did not characterize individuals by their sexual practices or desires, and the distinction between hetero- and homosexual did not exist. Since desire was not a moral object, the liberation of desire, a salient theme in the West since the 1920s, was not a political issue. The (free male) Greeks were different because the question of sexuality was placed in the register of the free activity of the individual to constitute himself. In short, sex was an aesthetic question, a matter of life-style.

If Foucault's depiction of Greek sexuality is convincing, one can see how sharp is the break between it and modern sexuality. His personal and political interest in gay liberation, even granting his reservations about the movement, is strongly supported by his argument, although he places no special value on the Greek love of boys or, better, precisely because he does not do so. The power of his analysis derives from its ability to constitute the past as different, not as an alternative to the present, an option for current political strategy. Such a project could be accomplished only by presenting the past in its specificity, ascetically reducing its ideological function to the minimum of difference itself. To raise Greek sexuality to the status of a standard for the present, to advocate the love of boys as a political focus today, would destroy the critical value of the work. That is precisely what Marxist historians do when they glorify the heroic struggles of the proletariat of previous times or present the trials of the working class in tones of unrelenting horror. The value of Foucault's *History of Sexuality* for critical theory lies precisely in its ascetic denial of teleology, its sharp constraint on rationalist universalism, and its genealogical presentation of difference.

The precise object constituted by Foucault as his historical field is "the forms and modalities of the relation to self by which the individual is constituted and recognizes himself as subject" (12). Characteristically, Foucault does not spend much time defining his categories of analysis, in this case *self* and *subject*. It appears from the text that *self* is a neutral, ahistorical term, almost a synonym for "individual." *Subject* is an active, historical term that refers to a process of interiorization. Foucault, of course, continues to reject philosophies of consciousness by which the individual ontologically constitutes him- or herself through mental activities.[12] Still, there is some ambiguity in Foucault's use of the term *subject*. It is not always clear that he consistently avoids a "subjectivist" use of it, especially in volumes 2 and 3 of *The History of Sexuality*, where the text often reads like a conventional intellectual history in which the paraphrase of one Greek thinker's ideas follows that of another. The verification of this complaint can safely be left to the reader, since it is a judgment based on the characterization of long sections of the texts and cannot be demonstrated by a selection of quotations or citations.

Foucault's apparent intention, if I may use that word, is to define the subject experientially and historically. The key to understanding this use of the term *subject* is his Nietzschean concept of truth. Since Foucault rejects the notion of absolute truth he also rejects the concept of the subject as source or foundation of truth. His notion of the subject is both decentered and relativist. The subject takes shape through historically experienced discourses/practices. In this way the role of sex in the constitution of the self as subject becomes clear. It appears that the overall project of *The History of Sexuality* is to trace the path, by no means a straight one, through which individuals become, in the modern period, subjects whose truth is their sexuality. If that is the case, the place of the Greeks in the historical trajectory takes on new meaning.

---

[12]Foucault discusses this question briefly in "Le retour de la morale," p. 41.

From the perspective of the history of the subject, the Greeks are not so much a point of difference as a point of origin. The rudiments of the modern subject can be traced to the Greek problematization of the self in the practice of the love of boys. Sex becomes a moral problem for the Greeks of the fourth to the second centuries B.C. because the passive positioning of free males contradicts the ethics of freedom. The Greek masters caught themselves in a conundrum that was creative. In wrestling with their dilemma over the love of boys they gave birth to the subject. Only in this sense does sex play a role in Foucault's history of the Greeks.

It must be admitted that Foucault is not entirely convincing on this issue. Everything seems to hinge on the identification of sexual penetration with "activity" and activity with freedom, also on the identification of being sexually penetrated with passivity and passivity with slavery.[13] In *L'usage des plaisirs* Foucault writes that the young man's honor "depends in part on the use he makes of his body . . . which will also to some extent determine his reputation and his future role" (235). As a free citizen he will be judged by his ability to lead a dignified and beautiful life. If the boy allows himself to be the passive object of another's pleasure he will not be able to command the respect necessary to a master. And yet it is not at all clear that in the sexual relationship the boy is any more an object of another's pleasure than is the adult. Foucault relies on the work of historians of Greece to determine that such was indeed the case for the ancients.[14] But the determination of the fact of the passivity of Greek boys in sexual relations with adult males does not resolve the interpretive question of why it was so. Foucault apparently assumes that a sexual relationship in which one partner is required to play an *exclusively* active role and the other

---

[13]Foucault does not mention penetration as a factor until vol. 3, p. 43, which is most peculiar since it is implied throughout vol. 2. He discussed sexual penetration earlier in Michel Foucault and Richard Sennett, "Sexuality and Solitude," *Humanities in Review* 1 (1982), 16, where he characterized the change from Greek to Christian technologies of the self: "The main question of sexual ethics has moved from the relations to people, and from the penetration model to the relation to oneself and to the erection problem." Erection symbolized all involuntary sexual impulses and led to a concern for internal purification, whereas penetration expressed social relations and a concomitant sexual ethic.

[14]Foucault, in a review of the French translation of *Greek Homosexuality* by Kenneth James Dover (London: Duckworth, 1978), notes with praise the author's discussion of the question of activity and passivity in Greek social and sexual relations. I am indebted to David Hoy for showing me this review, which appeared in *Libération*, June 1, 1982, p. 27.

partner to play an *exclusively* passive role is possible, as if the fact of "activity" and "passivity" were not ambiguous from the start, as if the Greek *interpretation* of the sexual relationship of man and boy as one of "activity" and "passivity" can be noted as an observation by the historian and left at that.

Foucault never asks, although it seems necessary to do so, why the Greeks attributed a passive role to the boys in the sexual relationship but never doubted the active role of the adult males. In the absence of such an interrogation the locus of the problematization of sex in the love of boys is thrown into doubt. From Foucault's description of the detailed elaboration of the practice of the love of boys there is little reason to question his argument that that relationship was indeed the problematic one for the Greeks. What is in question, however, is why that was so. It is possible that the man-boy sexual relationship was problematic to the men not simply because the boy's "passive" role contradicted their later position of dominance but also because in that relationship a reversal of roles was always possible. The man might at some moments be in a "passive" position physically or emotionally, and the boy might be in the "active" position. Sexual relations are certainly volatile and ambiguous, especially if their emotional side is taken into account. That indeed might be the great lacuna of Foucault's history of sexuality: a relative and remarkable absence of discussion about the affective nuances of sexual relationships.

Foucault's reticence about the emotional side of sex is difficult to comprehend. Certainly he is interested in the constitution of the self, not in sex per se. Even if that is granted, one can still question his repression of the question of the complex emotionality inherent in the issue of the constitution of the self. Perhaps the reason for the omission lies in Foucault's aversion to Freudian discourse, laden as it is with the question of conscious and unconscious feelings. Indeed, one could imagine a Freudian interpretation of the Greek love of boys that would differ considerably from Foucault's, throwing into question the larger framework of his work. A Freudian might see in the Greek love of boys an ambiguous sexual identity on the part of the adult males, an interpretation that presupposes a fixed libido and therefore precludes the kind of historical interpretation of sex Foucault is after. Foucault, of course, rejects a Freudian interpretation of the history of sexuality; that much is clear from volume 1. So it is perhaps unfair to raise this objection. In any case this unresolved difficulty casts a shadow of doubt over volume 2 of *The History of Sexuality*.

During the first two centuries A.D., Foucault contends, important changes occurred in the place of sex in the constitution of the self. In *Le souci de soi* Foucault discusses these changes by analyzing certain texts of the period, especially those of the stoic Epictetus. Volume 3 is much drier than volume 2, containing much more paraphrase and less analysis. Also, the significance of the changes that occurred during the period is presented somewhat ambiguously. Some of the texts reveal little change; others more. Foucault seems to pick his way carefully—some would say arbitrarily—through them, cautiously outlining the new configuration. The result is that the outlines of the new shape of sex are drawn lightly and easily recede into a shapeless chaos.[15] Yet in Foucault's opinion the most important single change in the entire history of sex in the West occurred during this period: there emerged a prohibition against the love of boys along with a rising valuation of heterosexual love.[16]

In the passage from ancient Greece to Hellenistic Rome the major change concerning sexuality was a shift of emphasis from the love of boys to the marriage tie. In order to comprehend this change properly Foucault describes a more general transformation that affected the masters. In the Greek period the free male individual was preoccupied with controlling or managing his desires. He sought an ideal of moderation, which was thought to enhance his freedom. In the first two centuries A.D. the emphasis shifted to what Foucault calls "the culture of self," an intensification of concern with "the relation to self." Foucault speaks of the change as the attainment of the "apex of a curve" rather than as a rupture.[17] He relates the new preoccupation with self to the altered political circumstances. No longer directly in command of society, the elite under the Roman Empire was an administrative class. In the new political system, Foucault surmises, the rules of the game made it more difficult for the individual male to attain a stable identity or to define the relations through which the subject was constituted. Political activity was more problematic, throwing the individual into a certain doubt about himself. One's position depended on signs that were more difficult to grasp than under the smaller city-

[15]For two eloquent statements of opposing views, see Michael Ignatieff's review of vols. 2 and 3 in *TLS*, September 28, 1984, pp. 1071–72; and David Hoy's review of recent Foucault literature in *London Review of Books*, November 1–14, 1984, pp. 7–9.

[16]Foucault does not stress this point in the text, but he related it to me in a conversation we had in Paris in July 1981.

[17]Foucault, *Le souci de soi* (Paris: Gallimard, 1984), p. 59, hereafter cited parenthetically in the text. Translations are my own.

states of earlier times. Hence the individual needed to scrutinize his actions much more carefully.

The emphasis on marriage developed in the imperial context. As the political institution became more "public," more complex, marriage became more "private" and in turn more "important, intense, difficult and problematic" (96). Men sought a new, more equal and more personal relationship with their wives than had the Greeks. Marriage became a "symmetrical bond," rendering the sexual relations of husband and wife problematic and intense.

"The woman-wife was valorized as the other par excellence; but the husband had also to recognize her as forming a unity with self. In comparison to traditional forms of matrimonial relations, the change was considerable" (192). In place of the elaborate subculture surrounding the love of boys, the wife became the center of the man's sexuality and accordingly the locus in which he constituted his subjectivity.

In the new situation an effort was made for the first time to develop a universal ideal of the subject. Nature and reason became standards by which to judge and evaluate the individual's realization of the culture of self. Implicit in the universalization of the sexual subject was an intensification of the forms of prohibition. Foucault emphasizes that we are still not at the level of constraint that obtained in the Christian period, with its elaborate codes and punishments. Still, a kind of threshold had been crossed during the early Roman Empire. Sex, while not considered intrinsically evil or even bad, was seen as the source of many serious dangers for the self. The focus on the marital tie implied increasing avoidance of intercourse with boys or servants. Extramarital relations were not, strictly speaking, prohibited, but they became an area of question for the culture of the self. In sum, the Hellenistic period witnessed a shift in sexual objects, an intensification of prohibitions concerning sexuality, and a deepening subjectification of the self.

Le souci de soi manifests a loosening of the grip Foucault has on his theoretical strategy. His presentation of the constitution of the self in the Hellenistic period falls short of the level of analysis that characterized his earlier work. The problem can be clearly seen if the text is evaluated as an example of archaeology.[18] Foucault mentions the term

---

[18]It has been argued that Foucault gave up the strategy of archaeology in the early 1970s. This is the position of Hubert Dreyfus and Paul Rabinow, in *Michel Foucault:*

archaeology only once in volumes 2 and 3 of *The History of Sexuality*. In *L'usage des plaisirs* he explains the purpose of the volumes in terms of archaeology and genealogy and in relation to the corpus of his work:

The archaeological dimension of the analysis permits the analysis of the forms themselves of problematization; its genealogical dimension permits the analysis of their formation starting from practices and their modifications. The problematization of madness and illness starting from social and medical practices defines a certain profile of "normalization." The problematization of life, language and work in discursive practices follows certain "epistemic" rules. The problematization of crime and criminal behavior starting from certain punitive practices follows a "disciplinary" model. And now I would like to show how in Antiquity sexual activity and pleasures were problematized through practices of self, setting into play criteria of an "aesthetic of existence." [17–18]

In *Madness and Civilization, The Birth of the Clinic, The Order of Things*, and *Discipline and Punish*—the works Foucault refers to here, all but one of which were written before the elaboration of the methods of archaeology and genealogy—Foucault achieved considerable success in accomplishing his goals. Can the same be said of *The History of Sexuality*?

In *The Archaeology of Knowledge* Foucault outlines a method of analyzing texts which sets aside the intentions of the authorial subject. He asks how the "statements" in a given discourse are possible. His theoretical strategy is, by working within the texts themselves, to develop an analysis of the text as discourse, as an objective field of positions or statements. This analysis proceeds at a level beneath that of the consciousness of the author, hence the term *archaeology*. *Discipline and Punish* locates the disciplinary statements in discourses on punishment even though the writers, like Jeremy Bentham, were motivated to establish methods for the rehabilitation of criminals, not to institute systems of discipline. In this method, everything hinges on the ability of the critic to go beyond the intentional level of the discourse to locate a system of problematics at once outside the text and within it, which, when elaborated, reveals a new level of significance in the text.

Beyond Structuralism and Hermeneutics (Chicago: University of Chicago Press, 1982). But I do not think that is the case in light of his use of the term in *L'usage des plaisirs*. The history of Foucault's texts does not follow a linear pattern punctuated by clear and final breaks. He seems, rather, from time to time to return to certain themes, methods, and problems that one thought he had dropped for good.

Foucault's method works pretty well in *L'usage des plaisirs*; the problematization of sex, specifically the love of boys, in relation to the constitution of the self captures the texts of the ancients at a new level and displaces their intentional meaning. But in *Le souci de soi* things do not turn out as well for Foucault. The difference is subtle, perhaps remaining an ambiguous question of interpretation. At issue are not the changes Foucault outlines in the history of sex and in the shape of the constitution of the self. The question is whether these changes are presented through archaeological and genealogical analyses. I think not, and I think not because the *Le souci de soi* reads like a traditional study in the history of ideas, relying too heavily on the intentional level of meaning, direct arguments, and explicit phrases of the author. *Le souci de soi* does not seem to get beyond an Aristotelian reading that combines summary and argument; it simply rearranges these sorts of readings to construct the analysis Foucault desires to make. And if that is so, Foucault leaves himself open to traditional methods of critique which might ask if he forces the text to yield the meaning he wants, if he selects texts only because they display positions that conform to his "bias" and interpretation, and so forth. These are questions for empiricist historians to ask. From the perspective I am pursuing—the adequacy of Foucault's position for a reconstituted critical theory—the problem is different. For me, the inadequacy of the archaeological level of interpretation explains, I think, the failure of the text to further the development of critical theory.

One example will suffice to make my case. Foucault argues, as we have seen, that there is a shift in the locus of problematization of sex from the love of boys to the marriage tie. He finds traces of the change in the writings of Musonius. "It is in Musonius that one finds articulated in the greatest detail the principle of symmetrical, conjugal fidelity" (201). And further on, "This integral conjugalization of sexual practice that one finds in Musonius, and the principle of a strict monopoly of *aphrodesia* reserved for marriage, are no doubt exceptional" (202). The reader finds a detailed description of Musonius's position, presented at the level of what he says in the text; the meaning of the text conforms to the change argued for by Foucault; the unrepresentative status of the text is announced by Foucault. The genealogical level of "practices and their modifications" is not a problem. Foucault does little with the level of practices in this text; yet what he writes about the emergence of a "culture of self" appears to be sound. The archaeological level, on the contrary, never seems to be reached. The objectivist level of reading statements in texts is forgotten in favor of a recitation of what the author says.

Nonetheless the change outlined by Foucault from the Greek constitution of the self through discourses on the sexual practice of the love of boys to the Christian constitution of the self through elaborate restrictive codes against the pleasures of the flesh is a dramatic and fascinating story. Foucault has again presented a fresh and vigorous interpretation of an obscure topic. The completion of his project with volumes carrying the history forward to modern times would certainly have resulted in a most important statement and remains a task for others. Based on what has been done in volumes 1 through 3 it is possible to draw the main lines of such a history or at least to suggest one direction the story might take.

Like Nietzsche, Foucault sees the main historical rupture occurring with Christianity. For Nietzsche all morality since the Christian epoch has been a set of variations on that slave morality. For Foucault the basic technique of the self of the last eighteen hundred years was developed by the Christians. They instituted an elaborate code, universally applicable, to regulate sexual conduct and thoughts. They based the code on a principle of the sinful nature of the flesh. They established a practice of confession through which their discourse on sex governed social action and thought. And above all they established sex as the truth about the self. The coupling of truth and sex was an innovation that would endure through all the profound changes discourse would undergo in the modern period. Starting in the eighteenth century, when discourses on sex began to appear in a rationalist and then scientific register, the same coupling of truth and sex would persist. As Foucault argued in *Le volonté de savoir*, the past two centuries have witnessed an increasing proliferation of discourses on sex—the writings of medical men in the eighteenth and nineteenth centuries, the formation of psychoanalysis in the late nineteenth century, the multiplication of sex therapies and research in the late twentieth century—all sharing the premise that some deep truth about the individual was bound up with sexuality.

If the foregoing serves as an admittedly crude outline of how the history of sex might proceed along lines traced by Foucault, certain limitations of the project need briefly to be mentioned, especially two areas in which contemporary sex is implicated but which do not appear to fit neatly into Foucault's scheme. The first is the increasing diminution of social networks in the context of the mode of information. As electronic systems are substituted, at all points of the social field, for face-to-face communications, individuals experience and are subject to new linguistic experiences. The relation of discourse to practice is profoundly changed. It is not clear that Foucault's theoretical strategy is adequate for an analysis of, for example, television advertising, which in many cases attempts to coordinate the consumption of commodities with sexual fantasies. Some type of semiological theory appears to be more appropriate, a theory that can unpack the linguistic mechanisms at play in the linguistic communication of television advertising.

The other area in which Foucault's method seems inappropriate but which is crucial to the constitution of the self in sex is the family. When Foucault treats the family he does so through systems of discourse which are external to it but act upon it, most notably that of the medical profession. The family, however, is also constituted internally through the constellation of interactions, especially at the emotional level, among its members. Only a psychological theory can adequately grasp these phenomena, but Foucault ignores or is critical of psychology. In sum, *The History of Sexuality* opens a new level of understanding, but it is unclear if its completion would have fully satisfied the requirements of a critical theory of sex.

6

Foucault, Poststructuralism, and the Mode of Information

In the United States poststructuralism is commonly understood in the context of literary criticism, but in this chapter I treat it as a response to the crisis of Marxism. Poststructuralism is illuminated in a new way when it is seen in relation to the inability of classical Marxism to serve as a critical theory of advanced industrial society. The positions of poststructuralism are significant to the extent that they present a critique of Marxism and therefore indicate the paths that may be taken to get beyond its current theoretical impasses. My aim, therefore, is to take poststructuralism as far as it can go in the critique of Marxism and then to outline its own limitations as a critical theory. In this effort I take Foucault's work as the main reference point, since, of all the poststructuralists, he has been most concerned with the problems of historical materialism.

Marxism centers critical theory and it totalizes from that center. In the essay "The Jewish Question," Marx presents a critique of the liberal solution to the project of human emancipation. He argues that the liberal version of emancipation is flawed because it is limited to political emancipation. What is needed, he thinks, is a form of emancipation which encompasses civil society as well as politics, the private sphere as well as the public. Only in that way can domination be thoroughly eliminated. He finds the key to human emancipation in the organization of labor and in the potential critical praxis of the working class. In short, the foundation of Marxism is a revised project for "total human emancipation" which is centered on the working class. It is a tribute to Marx's consistency that he never surrendered this project or compromised its integrity. From the *1844 Manuscripts* through *The German Ideology* and *Capital*, the basic principle of social critique remained the same: only the working class can abolish capitalism and therefore abolish the distinction between the private and the public, along with all the forms of domination that divide society into classes and prevent the formation of community. The totalization of critique at the locus of the working class remains the keystone of Marx's thinking through all the shifts of position or "breaks" that one may wish to locate in it.

Foucault and the poststructuralists take exception to the formal aspects of Marx's critique, to its centering and totalizing tendencies. They do not think critical theory can find its center in the working class or that it should busy itself with searching for a center in any case. The history of socialist and capitalist societies in the twentieth century provides all the evidence one could want to dispute the claim that the working class is the unique vanguard of "total emancipation." More important to the critique of Marx is the poststructuralist's admonition that centers of discourse serve to repress unwanted questions and to disqualify valid objections.

Foucault took two positions on this question. During the heyday of the "new philosophers" in the mid-1970s he gave more credence than was warranted to the anti-Gulag craze, flirting with a position that was barely distinguishable from anticommunism. At that point Foucault rejected Marx as a totalitarian thinker. But in other moments he acknowledged the critical force of Marxism if it could be understood as the special, not the general theory of the working class and its wrongs.[1] The main thrust of Foucault's writings is to admit that capitalism exploited and alienated the proletariat but at the same time to insist that other social groups also suffered domination, that these forms of domination could not be understood from the perspective of the categories developed to reveal the domination of the working class, and finally that in the context of advanced capitalism it was likely that forms of domination suffered by groups outside the workplace were better locations from which to initiate revolutionary movements than was the factory.

---

[1]See, for example, the interview "Prison Talk," in *Power/Knowledge: Selected Interviews and Other Writings, 1972–1977*, ed. Colin Gordon, trans. Colin Gordon et al. (New York: Pantheon, 1980), pp. 37–54.

The insane (in *Madness and Civilization*), prisoners (in *Discipline and Punish*), homosexuals (in *The History of Sexuality*), and women (in *The History of Sexuality* and *The Birth of the Clinic*) are groups that were constituted in dominated positions by the discourses/practices of modern society and whose domination is obscured, not illuminated, by the theory of the mode of production. Indeed, in the aftermath of May 1968 the momentum of radicalism had shifted away from the working class. The focuses of protest in the 1970s were feminism, gay liberation, antipsychiatry, prison reform—the groups addressed by Foucault's writings—as well as other challenges to capitalism which were equally at the margins of the theory of the mode of production (racial, ethnic, and regional protest; antinuclear movements; ecologists; and so forth). Thus poststructuralism argues for a plurality of radical critiques, placing in question the centering of critical theory in its proletarian site.

In a similar vein, poststructuralism disputes the tendency of Marxism to limit critical theory to a given center. The quest for a unique center is the bane of both Foucault and Derrida, though their intentions are quite distinct if not at odds. For the poststructuralists, theories that rely on a center are burdened by the limitations of reductionism. In the *1844 Manuscripts* Marx recognized the difficulty quite sharply. He admonished those thinkers who persist in positing questions of origin:

If you ask about the creation of nature and man, you thus abstract from man and nature. You assert them as *non-existent* and yet want me to prove them to you as *existing*. I say to you: Give up your abstraction and you will also give up your question. Or if you want to maintain your abstraction, be consistent and if you think of man and nature as *non-existent*, think of yourself as non-existent as you too are nature and man. Do not think, do not question me, for as soon as you think and question, your *abstraction* from the existence of nature and man makes no sense.[2]

The question of origin or center exceeds the proper limits of reason and is therefore fruitless. When a social theorist specifies an absolute origin, he or she denies the differential forces at play in all beginnings, which operate to relativize origins. The theorist posits a privileged status for him- or herself as well as for the object specified. This privilege is metaphysical. Thus to maintain the question of origin is to inflate reason to a degree that invalidates its critical function. And yet

[2]*Writings of the Young Marx on Philosophy and Society*, ed. and trans. Lloyd Easton and Kurt Guddat (New York: Anchor, 1967), pp. 313–14.

only two years later, in *The German Ideology* of 1846, Marx proposes to discover the origin of class society in the division of labor. The division of labor "alienates" human beings from their universality or species being; they equate their particular position in the division of labor with the general good, falsely identifying their particular interests with the general interest. History begins as the alienation of species being in the division of labor and will end only with the onset of communism, which puts an end to the division of labor. A center was thus proposed for revolutionary theory—labor—and it would remain installed in that theory through the nineteenth and twentieth centuries, sitting there, the poststructuralists would say, in a disruptive relationship with radicalism, functioning to limit the boundaries of critique.

It is not a long step from the concept of the center to that of totalization. Theories that maintain a center also totalize. The problems introduced by totalizations are no less severe than those of the center. Totalizations are always reductive. In addition they have a feedback effect that positions the totalizing theorist in a stance of domination. Critical theory seeks to assist the movement of revolution by providing a counterideology that delegitimizes the ruling class. In a curious manner, however, revolutionary theory itself tends to become a point of domination in the historical field. In Leninism, for example, the locus of theory is the locus of leadership and eventually the locus of bureaucratic control. The totalizing tendency in Marxist thought thus slips into the totalitarian power of the Marxist state. I do not wish to assert a causal relationship between a feature of theory (totalization) and a social system (totalitarianism). The forces at work in the creation of the Soviet state apparatus were complex and overdetermined. Nevertheless the tendency toward totalization in theory does counteract the praxis of democratizing social movements. In these cases, theory becomes the point of certainty for the movement; the informing function of theory becomes a directing function.

The problem of totalization is not as easily eliminated from theory as the poststructuralists would imply. An aspect of totalization necessarily emerges in every effort to counter the prevailing ideology and appears to be necessary to the process of thought itself. Derrida's otherwise careful strategy of deconstruction, for example, which strives to posit nothing except rigorous textual analysis, becomes itself a totalization, excluding all other positions in spite of itself.[3] It appears

[3]See, for example, Jacques Derrida, *Of Grammatology*, trans. Gayatri Spivak (Baltimore: Johns Hopkins University Press, 1976).

that Sartre was on the right track in the opening pages of *The Critique of Dialectical Reason* when he attempted to present a social phenomenology of totalization.[4] Consciousness totalizes its field as surely as totalization inhibits the freedom of the totalizer. The act of formulating a problem implies the decision that other problems will not be addressed. In that sense there has occurred a totalization of the field of possible problems to theorize. Contrary to the positions of the poststructuralists there is no antidote to totalization, no simple theoretical step that can completely eliminate its force and effects.[5]

Nonetheless much can be done to curtail and inhibit the limiting effects of totalizing thought. Along this line Foucault has proposed a distinction between the "universal" and the "specific" intellectual. In addition to the problem of totalizing theory, the figure of the universal intellectual is a subject of serious critique of Marx by the poststructuralists. Foucault argues that Marxist intellectuals may be termed "universal" in the sense that they claim to speak for humanity.[6] Marxists naturally do not speak for the bourgeoisie, but they claim that the proletariat embodies the interests of humanity and the hopes for a society without classes. This posture, Foucault contends, leads to severe difficulties for the movement of emancipation.

Since Foucault assumes a close connection between discourse and power, he finds a danger in the arrogation of power by the universal intellectual. Also the claim to speak for the universal can be troublesome because it denies the multifarious oppressions that Foucault assumes to be a feature of contemporary society. In place of the universal intellectual, Foucault discerns the specific intellectual emerging since World War II. Closely associated with a particular form of oppression in a particular institution, the specific intellectual is less likely to take control of the protest movement and less likely to reduce all forms of domination to that of his or her constituency.[7] In this way the pretensions of Marxist political parties to represent the entire Left are undercut. Foucault recognizes the dangers of pluralism and anar-

[4]Jean-Paul Sartre, *Critique of Dialectical Reason*, trans. Alan Sheridan-Smith (London: New Left Books, 1976), pp. 45–48.

[5]On the importance of the concept of totality to Western Marxism, see Martin Jay, *Marxism and Totality* (Berkeley: University of California Press, 1984).

[6]Foucault, "Truth and Power," in *Power/Knowledge*, pp. 126–30.

[7]Foucault's categories are different from those of Antonio Gramsci, who distinguishes between organic and traditional intellectuals. Gramsci did not raise the question of theory as a form of domination, so that his organic intellectuals are both theorists and activists who have a direct link with the institution.

chism connected with the specific intellectual,[8] but at least the dangers of reductionism are minimized. A full evaluation of Foucault's concept of the specific intellectual requires an analysis of the social roles of intellectuals in the past few decades, an analysis that is beyond the scope of this chapter.

The third challenge to Marxism presented by poststructuralism, which I have developed as an elaboration of the poststructuralist position, concerns changes in the nature of contemporary society which are reflected in the thought of Foucault and Derrida but also illuminated by their thought. Like many other twentieth-century thinkers, Foucault and Derrida are centrally concerned with language. In Derrida's texts the category of *écriture*, or writing, is the point of departure for an entire critical position. While writing is but one form of language, Derrida sees certain features of it as characteristic of all language. From the standpoint of this chapter what is important is the preoccupation with language as opposed to action. And Derrida takes a certain structure he finds in writing as the basis for a critique of the Western philosophical tradition, of the "logocentrism" that underlies thinking even in the revolutionary camp.

Foucault, too, takes a certain view of language as the heart of critique, one that he calls discourse. For him Western thought since Descartes has assumed the innocence of reason. By focusing on discourse instead of on ideas, Foucault demonstrates the linkage of knowledge and power. Without pursuing the subtleties of the poststructuralists' position any further, I can conclude that they ground their critiques in forms of linguistic experience, as opposed to forms of consciousness or forms of action. The focus on language constitutes an important shift in discursive strategy, which raises the question of context. What are the conditions for this shift and how may it be understood?

If we inquire into the changes of linguistic experience in the recent past, it becomes apparent that beneath the philosophical project of the poststructuralists a new linguistic world has appeared in social life. For what characterizes advanced capitalism is precisely a sudden explosion of multiple types of linguistic experience at every point in daily life. The act of production, for one, is increasingly defined by computer-regulated machines. The world of leisure, as well, increasingly concerns the manipulation of information processors. Social control

---

[8]Foucault, "Truth and Power," p. 130.

systems are dependent on vast amounts of stored information and on organizations that can manipulate that information. Knowledge about the social world is indirectly transmitted from one person to another through the mediation of electronic devices. Science once presented itself as standing outside the world of opinion, as the rational critique of ignorance and the domination that ensued from it. Now science and reason are part of the machinery of society and participate in the systems of social control and domination. To avoid obsolescence critical theory must account for the line of new languages that stretches from body signals, grunts, spoken language, and writing to print, the telegraph, radio, film, television, computers, and other new linguistic technologies. These new phenomena constitute a rupture with traditional linguistic experience, and they make possible new forms of communicative relationships. It is reasonable to hypothesize that the network of social relations is being fundamentally altered at the present time by the new linguistic experiences.

The poststructuralists do not often reflect on the social world in which their positions are developed. But those positions are symptoms of the times and are useful in comprehending the emerging social formation. If Marx omitted a language theory when he analyzed the change from feudalism to capitalism, such an absence is no longer tolerable. The change from capitalism to late capitalism or from the mode of production to what I call the mode of information requires the reconstitution of critical theory, a reformulation that can unlock the forms of domination inherent in diverse linguistic experiences, reveal the significance of new forms of protest particular to the present conjuncture and imagine the shape of a democratic future that is possible as a transformation of the present situation.

Foucault's *Discipline and Punish* exemplifies the advances and hesitations of poststructuralism in relation to the mode of information. The book presents a detotalized view of the social field. It examines the formation of new mechanisms of punishment without ontologizing that mode of domination as the key to total freedom or the "riddle of history." *Discipline and Punish* traces the emergence of a new "technology of power" in the nineteenth century without claiming that it is the base upon which everything else rests, without consigning histories of other aspects of the nineteenth century to the status of epiphenomena or superstructures. Relations between the new technology of power (the panopticon) and other social levels such as the economy are described without any hint of reductionism. Capitalism is not reduced to the panopticon; instead, the complex play of their interactions is given due recognition. Metaphysics is kept at bay as well when Foucault traces the origins of the panopticon. The new technology of punishment emerges in the nineteenth century out of a complex play of differential forces. The difference between the panopticon and torture (the earlier system of punishment) is not absolute. Unlike Marx in his analysis of the origins of the division of labor, Foucault does not present the birth of the prison as the institution of domination in human history, as the beginning of human alienation. Instead, he goes to great lengths to show that the torture system included a strong element of domination, so that the change to the panopticon constitutes a substitution of one system of domination for another, a relative, not an absolute transformation. At the same time he undermines the opposite metaphysical strategy, that of liberals who view the change as one from evil to good. For liberalism the birth of the prison signifies decisive progress in the dignity and freedom of man. The panopticon abolished ''cruel and unusual punishments'' and was decisive proof that liberal society had inaugurated the reign of freedom on earth. On the contrary, Foucault indicates, first, that while the torture system was certainly cruel, it was a coherent mechanism of social control, not the incarnation of evil. Similarly, the prison system, while it rid society of cruel spectacles of punishment, instituted a new mechanism of power that was efficient and effective in controlling populations. In this way Foucault presents an origin (the panopticon was a genuinely new mechanism) that is free of metaphysics.

A third important feature of *Discipline and Punish* speaks to the advances of poststructuralism over traditional critical theory. In his analysis, Foucault integrates with critical theory the new sense of the importance of language. The depiction of the panopticon includes not only an institutional framework and a system of practices but also a set of discourses. These discourses consist of the Enlightenment reformers' tracts advocating the abolition of torture and the writings of Bentham and others proposing the basic form of the panopticon. It includes as well the records kept by the administrators of the prisons and by the police. Especially interesting, however, is the role of the discourse of the new science of criminology in the legitimation of the panopticon. Through a discussion of criminology Foucault demonstrates how the human sciences are implicated in systems of domination. He shows how discourses and practices are inextricably interwoven in the fabric of technologies of power, how science is not innocent of force. He offers the couplet discourse/practice to underscore the involvement of language with action. This sensitivity to the ability of language to shape practice is typical of the poststructuralists and exemplifies their rejection of the metaphysical dualism of mind and body, ideas and behavior, consciousness and action.

Yet with all these advances, Foucault and the poststructuralists do not take the next step in the deconstruction of traditional theory, a step that Marx himself pioneered. To avoid totalizing closure at the level of epistemology, to prevent one's own discourse from being regarded as an absolute beginning, in other words, as science, it is necessary to engage in the effort of self-reflection, to relativize one's status as a subject of knowledge. Foucault does entertain this line of thinking but he does so by systematically refusing to theorize. He chooses that strategy of deconstruction rather than the alternative of situating his discourse in its social-historical context. I will first analyze Foucault's effort at self-reflection and then offer an alternative that roots Foucault's discourse in the present conjuncture and thereby reveals a new level of analytical power.

Like Nietzsche, Foucault introduces his categories in the midst of his text without a full or systematic elaboration. For example, the concept of "technology of power," a central theme of *Discipline and Punish*, appears first on page 23 with no explanation whatsoever. Foucault is at that point discussing the "four general rules" of the book. The third rule reads as follows:

Instead of treating the history of penal law and the history of the human sciences as two separate series whose overlapping appears to have had on one or the other, or perhaps on both, a disturbing or useful effect, according to one's point of view, see whether there is not some common matrix or whether they do not both derive from a single process of "epistemological-juridical" formation; in short, make the technology of power the very principle both of the humanization of the penal system and of the knowledge of man.[9]

In this offhand manner Foucault specifies the object of his study as "the technology of power" of the prison systems from the old regime to the present. But what does it mean to say that one will "make the technology of power" the principle of both the institution of the prison and the social science that studies it? Foucault employs the term

[9]Foucault, *Discipline and Punish: The Birth of the Prison*, trans. Alan Sheridan (New York: Pantheon, 1977), p. 23.

technology of power dozens of times in the book; he also uses other terms as if they were identical to it in meaning ("micro-physics of power," "mechanisms of power," and so forth). At issue is not the game of finding all the meanings of *technology of power* in order to show a contradiction in Foucault's thought or simply to refine a formal definition of the term. The difficulty lies elsewhere: without a clearly enunciated systematic theory, the limits of Foucault's project remain uncertain. It is impossible to indicate the boundaries of the phenomenon of the technology of power, for instance, without a systematic elaboration of its conceptual basis. By the end of the book, the reader may have a pretty good notion of what Foucault means by the technology of power, but it will be very difficult indeed to determine if the category is compatible with other theories, such as Marxism, or if it can be the basis of studies of other institutional matrices. In fact, Foucault's tendency to totalize the concept technology of power, going against the grain of his general position, can be attributed to his failure adequately to theorize it.

There is a general tendency among poststructuralists to avoid formal theorizing. Derrida, much like Foucault, introduces new terms in each new book he writes. It may be retorted to my objection to the atheoretical strategy of the poststructuralists that they adopt such a strategy in order to avoid the very pitfalls of theorizing (such as totalization) that were addressed at the beginning of this essay. My response to that retort is that they have gone too far in the direction of antisystematic thinking and that an intermediate strategy needs to be developed by which categories are systematically developed without embedding them in a closed, totalizing system.

For his part, Foucault justifies his theoretical diffidence on the ground that it is required in order to develop a critique of the human sciences. He steadfastly rejects the traditional strategy of theoretical development and empirical verification that is practiced by liberal positivists and Marxists alike. In *The German Ideology* Marx insisted that the value of the theory of the mode of production could be determined only by empirical studies.[10] What Foucault finds objectionable in standard social science is the unacknowledged implication of the claim of knowledge, that is, the will to power. Like the Frankfurt School's critique of humanism in the *Dialectic of Enlightenment* and, of course, like Nietzsche in *Beyond Good and Evil*, Foucault argues that systematic

---

[10]*Writings of the Young Marx*, p. 431.

social science, especially careful theoretical elaboration, inherently contains an element of domination or a technology of power.[11] As Foucault stated in the passage where he introduces the term *technology of power*, the discourse of criminology is itself a form of power. Technologies of power consist of knowledge and practice intimately associated in the formation of social relations based on domination. Because social science is not neutral, above the fray of class struggles, the rational exercise of theoretical production is implicated in the problem of domination. And Marxism, with its oppressive state systems and hierarchical political parties is not different in principle from the behavioral sciences and public policy sciences of capitalism. Even if the theorist explicitly takes the side of the oppressed, rather than hiding behind the mask of scientific neutrality, the function of domination associated with systematic theory is not eliminated.

In *Discipline and Punish* Foucault is by and large consistent in his theoretical asceticism. Many readers find the book frustrating and difficult because while Foucault makes the case against modern prison systems, he offers nothing as a response to them. Some students of the book find in it deep despair[12] when this impression is better attributed to the effect on the reader of the convincing genealogy of prisons presented without the utopian alternative that systematic theory provides. Foucault himself replies to the charge of pessimism: "My point is not that everything is bad, but that everything is dangerous, which is not exactly the same as bad. If everything is dangerous, then we always have something to do. So my position leads not to apathy but to a hyper- and pessimistic activism."[13] This response to critics is inadequate not because it is untrue but because there is no ground in Foucault's text on which to base the conclusion of "hyper- and pessimistic activism." One may just as easily argue that the position emerging from *Discipline and Punish* is pessimistic apathy, optimistic adventurism, or whatever.

The reason that multiple, contradictory political conclusions are possible is that the concepts underlying the analysis of prison systems

---

[11]See Max Horkheimer and Theodor Adorno, *Dialectic of Enlightenment*, trans. John Cumming (New York: Seabury, 1972; orig. ed. 1944); Friedrich Nietzsche, *Beyond Good and Evil: Prelude to a Philosophy of the Future*, trans. Walter Kaufmann (New York: Vintage, 1966).

[12]See, for example, Edward Said, "Travelling Theory," *Raritan* (Winter 1982), 41–67.

[13]"How We Behave," interview with Michel Foucault, *Vanity Fair* (November 1983), 62.

are theoretically inchoate. If the concept of the technology of power were fully elaborated at some point in the text, a political stance of refusal would probably have to emerge as a clear conclusion. Forms of resistance to the technology of power, so underplayed by Foucault in the book (see his recognition of this problem in *Power/Knowledge*), are a necessary aspect of an analysis of the history of punishment systems from the perspective of critical theory.[14] Marx theorized a proletarian revolt against capitalism, and liberals theorized resistance to monarchical despotism. But if such a theoretical turn were taken, Foucault contends, the concept of technology of power would return to the theorist and become an emanation of the reason of the author, Foucault himself. The author of the theory would be the commander of a new movement and would exercise domination over its followers. The intellectual would take his place at the head of the revolutionary column; his mind would be venerated by the oppressed as a source of power, and they would be subject to oppression by him. Once again the scenario of the Western philosophical tradition would be enacted as Hegel's deity of reason would confirm its dialectical power of immanence.

Foucault's refusal of systematic theory is thus the poststructuralist's rejection of reason as the center of being. And Foucault gives up much to maintain that stance. He insists that his books are only tools for the revolutionary deconstruction of the established apparatus.[15] Alternatively, he would have us think of them as bombs for others to throw at the halls of power and wealth. The only systematic principle for this antisystematic writer is his denial of system, denial of reason, and necessarily denial of authorship.[16] Yet even if one sympathizes with Foucault's predicament or finds certain charms in the ambiguities of his writing, the position he is in remains a predicament, one fraught with difficulties.[17]

Discipline and Punish cannot escape its fate as a form of communication. However much Foucault would hide from his text, withdraw his authorship, and however sound his reason for doing so, his text

[14]For an attempt at a general theory of resistance, see Michel de Certeau, *The Practice of Everyday Life*, trans. Steven Rendall (Berkeley: University of California Press, 1984).

[15]*M. Foucault: Power, Truth, Strategy*, ed. Meaghan Morris and Paul Patton (Sydney: Ferral, 1979), p. 57.

[16]Foucault, "What Is an Author?" in *Language, Counter-Memory, Practice*, ed. Donald Bouchard (Ithaca: Cornell University Press, 1977), pp. 113–38.

[17]See the treatment of this problem by David Carroll, "The Subject of Archaeology of the Sovereignty of the Episteme," *Modern Language Notes* 93 (1978), 695–722.

remains itself a discourse, and as a discourse it retains its power effects. To deny them is not to make them go away. Foucault's confusion may have been, therefore, to think that his awareness of the limits of reason and systematic theory can result in a form of theory that is in a strange way not bound by those limits. In short, Foucault betrays an idealist assumption that an author's awareness of the dilemmas of authorship by itself avoids the difficulties or places one in a different relation to those difficulties or enacts those difficulties in the drama of the text, and thereby sanctions a stance of nonauthorship. Foucault implies that his mere awareness of the problem enables him, in his writing, to elude the technology of power inherent in writing. But it is clear that if the domination inherent in reason and authorship can be muted, that muting would occur not through an author's awareness but through a change in the social system, through a new set of practices in which the audience and the system of publishing no longer conferred power on the author, a situation that has probably never existed and may never exist. For these reasons the discourse of the technology of power must be considered badly incomplete and therefore open to a kind of misinterpretation beyond that inherent in the dialogic process of citation and reported speech.

If the story ended at this point a fundamental aspect of Foucault's achievement would remain obscured, that is, the epistemological advance of his position contained in the notion of discourse itself and, most important, the relationship of the concept of discourse to the mode of information. Earlier in this chapter I suggested that poststructuralism advances critical theory by raising the question of language, thereby opening the field of critical theory to the dramatic changes in linguistic experience which have so altered the social formation in the past few decades. At this point I will indicate how the poststructuralist position may be elaborated to account for the mode of information.

Critical theory has in general not looked favorably on positions rooted in theories of language, such as Foucault's concept of discourse. In *The German Ideology* Marx relegated language to an insignificant place in social theory: "From the start the 'spirit' bears the curse of being 'burdened' with matter which makes its appearance in the form of agitated layers of air, sounds, in short, in the form of language. Language is as old as consciousness. It *is* practical consciousness which exists also for other men and hence exists for me personally as well. Language, like consciousness, only arises from the need and necessity of relationships with other men."[18] This passage, one of the few where Marx directly speaks of language, has been interpreted in a manner that credits Marx with an awareness of the importance of language in society. He writes, after all, that language is "practical consciousness." Against this view I argue that in fact Marx is here dismissing the problematic aspect of language for critical theory. The emphasis in the passage as I read it is that language is determined by social relationships, that action precedes language. Support for my reading of the passage is found in the vast body of Marxist literature, which, with few exceptions, ignores the structuring features of language or at best treats language in the form of ideology as part of the superstructure.

For Marx the object of critical theory is praxis and in particular labor. The act of labor is the focus of social critique, and domination is revealed in the forms of the alienation and exploitation of the labor act. Even though praxis includes a moment of consciousness, the critique of domination focuses on the activity of labor. In fact the central object of the liberal tradition of the critique of domination also concerned a form of praxis. From John Locke onward, the main force of liberal criticism was brought to bear on arbitrary power, especially that of the monarch. In the liberal account, the acts of kings, nobles, and clerics were the source of the limits on freedom. In both liberal and Marxist traditions, emancipatory theory was grounded in the critique of action. Ironically, it was not until Stalin, a great tyrant and exploiter on his own, that Marxism began to consider language outside the framework of the superstructure, though other Marxists, such as Antonio Gramsci, had earlier registered criticisms of the base/superstructure distinction.

Recently Habermas and Baudrillard have attempted to base critical theory on forms of linguistic experience.[19] Habermas's concept of the ideal speech situation grounds the democratizing movement in an egalitarian context of public discussion in which reason may emerge. But "distorted communication," for Habermas, remains a product of the social relations of the speakers. His critique of domination does not

---

[18]*Writings of the Young Marx*, p. 421.

[19]For a more complete discussion of Baudrillard and Habermas on this question, see my "Technology and Culture in Habermas and Baudrillard," *Journal of Contemporary Literature* 22.4 (1981), 456–76. See also V. N. Volosinov, *Marxism and the Philosophy of Language*, trans. L. Matejka and I. Titunik (New York: Seminar Press, 1973).

yield categories for the analysis of the linguistic modes by which to reveal how language patterns are themselves sources of domination. Baudrillard's early work, especially *Towards a Critique of the Political Economy of the Sign* (1972), *The System of Objects* (1968), *Consumer Society* (1970), and *The Mirror of Production* (1973), move closer to a materialist theory of language.[20] His theory of the mode of signification was an effort to employ a variety of semiotic categories to disclose the domination inherent in linguistic forms in different epochs. Like Habermas, Baudrillard ran into difficulty over the question of utopia. He posited one linguistic form, that of the symbol, that promised liberation from the semiotic horrors of the code. Unlike Habermas, however, Baudrillard began the serious examination of contemporary modes of communication and significantly opened up the field of the semiology of everyday life.

Foucault's concept of discourse must be viewed in relation to this theoretical tradition if its advantages are to be grasped. First, Foucault rejected the split between knowledge and power, discourse and practice. Since, as Nietzsche had shown, knowledge was a form of power and since power created and shaped practice rather than limiting it, discourse was deeply implicated in the critique of domination. This strategy required that discourse be analyzed not as a form of consciousness, not as an expression of the subject, but as a form of positivity. The rejection of the subjectivity of discourse led Foucault in *The Archaeology of Knowledge* to elaborate a new set of categories that would allow discourse to stand on its own as a form of power: "I shall abandon any attempt . . . to see discourse as a phenomenon of expression—the verbal translation of a previously established synthesis; instead, I shall look for a field of regularity for various positions of subjectivity. Thus conceived, discourse is not the majestically unfolding manifestation of a thinking, knowing, speaking subject, but, on the contrary, a totality, in which the dispersion of the subject, and his discontinuity with himself may be determined."[21] This passage contains the rudiments of a concept of language, in the form of discourse, appropriate to a critical theory of the mode of information, one that, properly understood, remains materialist because it points to the analysis of modes of domination in the contemporary social field.

[20]For a fuller exploration of this topic, see Rosalind Coward and John Ellis, *Language and Materialism* (London: Routledge and Kegan Paul, 1977).

[21]Michel Foucault, *The Archaeology of Knowledge and the Discourse on Language*, trans. A. M. Sheridan-Smith (New York: Pantheon, 1972), p. 55.

Historical materialism is based on the conviction that the object of historical knowledge cannot be ideas because the ideas that people hold about social existence do not determine their existence. Marx formulated this salutary principle of interpretation at a time when historical thinking, especially in Germany, was indeed idealist. At that time, however, in the mid-nineteenth century, vast social changes were occurring in the organization of political and economic action. A theory grounded in idealism was particularly unsuited to lay bare the structures of these political and economic transformations.

But what must become of historical materialism at a time when the structures of linguistic experience are undergoing drastic change—when bureaucracies accumulate extensive files on the population; when visual and aural electronic impulses (television, telephone, radio, film) constitute significant portions of the communications in everyday life; when commodities are produced through the mediation of computers and sold through the mediation of clusters of meanings generated by advertising teams; when political processes are shaped by mass communication devices; when surveillance by the digital logic of the computer threatens to extend itself into every corner of the social world; when the human sciences and the natural sciences are integrated into the systems of social control and reproduction? In this mode of information, historical materialism must do more than calculate rates of exploitation and declining surplus value. It must do more than demonstrate the alienated conditions of the act of labor. Indeed, it must take into account these new forms of language; it must develop categories for the analysis of the patterns of domination and distortion inherent in their contemporary usage; and it must examine the historical stages of their development.

Employing only the traditional categories of Marxism (perhaps adjusted by the traditions of Western Marxism), one would learn how the new systems of language serve the ruling class and are controlled to some degree by them.[22] While that is a valid enterprise, it is not by itself adequate for the analysis of the mode of information. Foucault's late work is useful precisely on that account. *Discipline and Punish* avoids centering critical theory on a totalizing concept of labor. It grasps structures of domination in their specificity and, while relating different patterns of domination to one another, resists the temptation

[22]See Herbert Schiller, *Who Knows: Information in the Age of the Fortune 500* (New York: Ablex, 1981).

to reduce one to another. In addition the book employs a notion of discourse, further elaborated in *The History of Sexuality*, which sanctions the analysis of language, yet avoids grounding it in subjectivity. Critical theory thus has an example of an examination of a structure of domination in language which is not rooted in idealist assumptions. For these reasons, aspects of Foucault's methodology are valuable for a critical theory of the mode of information. Poststructuralism has come to the aid of critical theory not so much in the theory of writing as in the analysis of a digital logic that may relegate writing to past epochs of signifying practices.

Foucault himself did not situate his thought in relation to the new conjuncture. He did not define the present situation in terms of a new social formation, much less in terms of a mode of information or anything equivalent to it. As a result, the impact of his texts is less than it might be, and for several reasons. First, at the epistemological level he substitutes a strategy of evasion of authorial presence for that of situating his position in its historical conditions. Both strategies have the same intent: to undermine the absoluteness of the author as subject and origin of the text. But the former strategy, Foucault's, merely creates ambiguity over the interpretation of the text, while the latter, the one I am suggesting, more clearly defines the direction of political intervention the text proposes. On this score Foucault's tendency was to discuss his political positions in occasional pieces, interviews and the like, not in his major texts.

Second, if Foucault had specified those aspects of the social formation which provide the framework of the questions he posed, those questions and the works he developed to answer them could be more systematically developed into a critical theory. His texts would be part of a larger project and would not stand on their own, inviting critics to respond to them in terms of the star system of intellectuals. At the same time, to insert *Discipline and Punish* and other works into a theory of the mode of information would immeasurably clarify their conceptual underpinnings. Such notions as discourse/practice and technology of power would become specified in relation to particular levels of the social formation. By elaborating the concept of the mode of information in terms of new linguistic experiences, I have indicated the lines for this theoretical development. More work needs to be done in clarifying the concept of the mode of information, with particular attention to the question of avoiding totalization.

Third, by way of illustration, I will explore the analysis of the panopticon as presented in *Discipline and Punish* in relation to the mode of information. As a means of punishment and reform of criminals, the panopticon was a failure. As a means of control and discipline of a population, it was a success. Foucault, therefore, does not evaluate it in relation to juridical norms, as liberalism does, or in relation to the mode of production, as Marxism does. He treats it as a new technology of power peculiar to modern society. Its success as a tool of the administration of large institutions ensured its widespread use in schools, asylums, workplaces, the military, and so forth. The problem with Foucault's presentation is that it does not specify the characteristics of the social formation into which the panopticon is differentially inserted. For that reason, his analysis gets unhinged at points, and he takes positions that go against his own theoretical strategies. For example, at one point in the text he totalizes the panopticon as the general technology of power in modern society.[23] His refusal to specify the social formation derives from his reluctance to insert his writing into liberal or Marxist contexts, which would undermine the force of his analysis of the panopticon. But the alternative he takes, failure to specify the social formation, leads only to confusion.

He might have chosen a Weberian frame for his work.[24] After all, Weber is the theorist of bureaucratic society, in which the main issue of social control concerns the management of large populations. In addition, Weber presented a critique of the form of rationality associated with bureaucratic institutions and was the first major thinker, after Nietzsche, to associate reason (in the form of instrumental rationality) with domination, a strategy that Foucault himself admires a great deal. The chief drawback in Weber's position, and the reason why Foucault was prudent to avoid his standpoint, is that Weber fails to develop his position in relation to a theory of language; he limits himself to a theory of action. Weber's discourse remains rooted in the humanist dualism of reason and action. It is therefore unsuited to the task of reconstituting critical theory.

The only viable path open to Foucault would have been to develop his own sense of the social formation. Had he done so he might have recognized the extraordinary relevance of the discourse/practice of the panopticon in revealing new modes of domination. The panopticon's effectiveness was based on its ability to instill in each member of the

---

[23]Foucault, *Discipline and Punish*, pp. 216–17.
[24]He mentions and then rejects this path in a late interview. See "A Discussion of the Work of Michel Foucault," *Skyline* (March 1982), 18.

subject population the sense that they were always open to observation or surveillance by the administrative authorities. In the prison system of the nineteenth century this goal was accomplished largely by architectural means. A guard was positioned in a central tower with a complete circular view. Around him the cells were built so that the guard was able to see into them at his pleasure, but the prisoners were not able to ascertain whether they were being observed. The goal of the system was to so alter the prisoners awareness that they were to become continuously oriented to the prison authorities. One can easily imagine how this system might be effective not only in prisons but in other settings as well.

What Foucault apparently did not notice is that the same panoptical system has been perfectly and widely extended in the second half of the twentieth century by dint of the computer's ability to gather and store information. It is now possible to monitor large populations without the material apparatus of the nineteenth-century prison. Electronic monitoring of the population occurs silently, continuously, and automatically along with the transactions of everyday life. Under the domain of the superpanopticon the population need not be gathered in institutions to be observed. In the mundane affairs of private life as well as in public life the population is under the gaze of the corporate and state bureaucracies. Market behavior, personal preferences, credit status, vacation decisions, health profiles—every conceivable aspect of ordinary activity leaves a trace in the memory banks of machines, and these traces are available instantaneously should the occasion arise. The celebrated distinction, so dear to liberals, between private life and public life is being effectively abolished not by a communist revolution but by the extension of the panopticon as a technology of power.

Jeremy Bentham intended the nineteenth-century panopticon to instill in the prisoner a sense of omnipresent authority, to internalize in the criminal the sense of always being watched. This imposition of the other into the self was the first step in the reform of the offender. From that point on, Bentham hoped, the inmate's consciousness would be oriented toward society's moral system as embodied in figures of authority. The anonymous creators of the late twentieth-century superpanopticon may have had no similar intention. Yet the effect also concerns an alteration of the individual. Whether individuals are aware of it or not, the databases of the superpanopticon constitute a self for each individual, consisting of the sum of all the transactions registered by the individual. The individual in the super-panopticon may be unrecognizable by the individual in the flesh, but they are in effect one and the same. If Bentham's panopticon strove to alter the prisoner, to change one centered subject (the criminal) into another (the bourgeois), the superpanopticon supplements and complicates the self of the individual by constituting another self for that individual, one that may be as socially effective as the self that walks in the street.

Surveillance by the superpanopticon is made possible only by the mode of information. The new technology of power relies upon certain configurations of *linguistic* experience. Nothing illustrates better than the superpanopticon the interrelation of discourse and practice. Contemporary surveillance is a product of new methods of *information* processing, not brute force. What is needed, then, is a full analysis of new modes of linguistic experience in a manner that reveals the extent to which they constitute new modes of domination. It is difficult to see how critical theory can proceed without such an analysis. At the same time precautions must be taken to avoid totalizing the new theoretical direction. The aim must be to develop theoretically and to specify analytically the types of domination inherent in the mode of information.

Foucault's discussion of the panopticon leads directly into this theoretical line of inquiry but falls short of taking the important next steps. Poststructuralism has cleared the way for critical theory to incorporate the question of language. Only its undue suspicion of systematic theory and inadequate self-reflexivity prevents it from making a major theoretical breakthrough.

7

The Mode of Information

Electronic systems of communication are changing the fabric of advanced societies. A great historical upheaval is taking place, which promises to transfigure the structure of human interactions. What is going on today is comparable in significance to the industrial revolution of the nineteenth and early twentieth centuries. No one can predict what the future has in store, but one can imagine that, barring a nuclear conflagration, society in the year 2150 might be as different from that in 1950 as society in 1950 was from any other since the Stone Age.

We social scientists and historians are more than a little confused by what is taking place. Many insist that no radical changes are happening or will happen in the next decades. Some liberals see only a continuing, linear evolution in the shape of things. Computers and the like mean to them only increased efficiency in material production, a continuation of the substitution of machine for human labor which began with the industrial revolution or even with the appearance of human beings on earth. Some Marxists, clinging to the dialectic of the mode of production, persist in characterizing the advanced societies as capitalist and adamantly refuse to consider the possibility of a new epoch emerging in social relations. These social critics believe that arguments in favor of postindustrial or postmodern society ignore the fact of the endurance of capital and, worse, obscure the force of class domination.

A growing contingent of observers disagree with the timidity of these perspectives. There are analysts from all locations on the theoretical and political spectrum who discern enormous social transformations on the horizon. Many thinkers in this camp maintain that the computer will solve the vast majority of humankind's ills. A right-wing contingent envisions a benign automated world of material plenty, which will be achieved without structural changes in major institutions.[1] High technology alleviates toil and trouble, releasing workers for stimulating tasks. Political strife withers away as decisions are reduced to technical problems. A left-wing contingent, equally sanguine, foresees radical democracy as the outcome of the new technologies.[2] Obstacles to equality and creativity are displaced by humane social principles because the roots of oppression are embedded in the soil of primitive technology.

Positions in the debate are far more complex than I have indicated. Yet the basic issue at stake in the debate is a judgment about where we are going, a judgment that cannot be made on the basis of tables, graphs, and charts. The argument that postindustrial society has arrived is often based on the claim that more than 50 percent of the labor force is in the service sector.[3] These statistics are furiously refuted by those who reject the label "postindustrial." The contention that "the office of the future" will eliminate repetitive toil is disproved by demonstrating that high technology introduces far more tedious jobs than challenging ones. The prediction that daily life will be ameliorated by electronic communications is disputed with statistics that show only increasing isolation as a consequence of telephones, televisions, video recorders, stereos, and computers. To have the wider world at one's fingertips means to fragment the community into privatized cells. The notion that telecommunications eliminates distances between people and enables the instantaneous registration of individual preferences is countered with the warning that these same devices make possible the stability of ruling elites through techniques of surveillance. It appears that the choice among those who envision a radically different future due to the spread of electronic systems of communication is between wide-eyed techno-freaks with little sense of history and skeptics for whom *plus ça change, plus c'est la même chose.*

The concept of the mode of information, which designates a theoret-

[1]John Naisbitt, *Megatrends: Ten New Directions Transforming Our Lives* (New York: Warner, 1982).

[2]Yonegi Masuda, *The Information Society as Post-industrial Society* (Washington, D.C.: World Future Society, 1981; 1st ed. 1980).

[3]Daniel Bell, *The Coming of Post-industrial Society: A Venture in Social Forecasting* (New York: Basic Books, 1973).

ical break with earlier traditions of critical social theory, provides a way to move beyond the existing limits of debate. It provides a framework for isolating new features of the social landscape without pretending that older institutions have disappeared or even that they are in some sort of a minority position. The mode of information designates social relations mediated by electronic communication systems, which constitute new patterns of language. It is my hypothesis that an important new dimension of advanced society concerns language and can only be investigated by means of linguistically based concepts. The debate about postindustrial society proceeds from the faulty assumption that the measure of the social system is action. If people are *doing* the same things then society is the same. When secretaries use a computer terminal instead of a typewriter, they still perform the same task. If a worker performs a service task rather than works on an assembly line, he or she remains in a capital-labor relationship. The social order persists as long as there is economic growth or capital expansion. My argument, to the contrary, is that while all these claims are difficult to refute, their proponents are looking for changes in social action when in fact the important novelties emerge at the level of language.

The habits of social analysis run deep. It is difficult to escape from old conceptual patterns, from the long-held assumption that in the field of society action has priority over language. The theorists who established the contours of the study of society—Marx, Weber, and more ambiguously Emile Durkheim—all gave precedence to action over language. Marx stated his first assumption bluntly: human beings must *act* to satisfy their needs. For his part, Weber elaborated a theory of social *action* differentiated only by subjective states (means-and-ends rationality, traditionalism and emotion). These subjective states were grounded in forms of consciousness, not in language. While they disagreed on many important issues, the fathers of social science maintained a consensus on the fundamental assumption that action, not language, was the object of analysis.

In the twentieth century, two trends shake the position of the grand theorists. The first is the emergence of many theories of language—from Ferdinand de Saussure's and Noam Chomsky's to Ludwig von Bertalanffy's and J. L. Austin's—theories that enable a systematic analysis of linguistic phenomena beyond the mere study of changes in the meanings of words. The second trend is the introduction of new technologies—telegraph, telephone, radio, television, computer, communications satellite—which alter the time and space relations of communicators, manipulate the relation of sender and receiver of messages, transform the codes of language, in short, revolutionize the elements in the process of communication and the nature of language. These historical changes require the social sciences to reverse their priorities by giving new attention to linguistic experiences.

Language and action are interrelated aspects of experience. In fact, language may be considered a form of action and action is accompanied by linguistic expressions. By employing the term *mode of information* I do not want to suggest that in the social field language is separate from action or that it can be reified and considered as a self-subsisting totality. Quite the contrary: on this issue I follow Foucault's formulation of the term *discourse/practice*, by which he endeavors to bypass the traditional distinction between language and action, ideas and material things. Such a dualism obscures the way social experience is concurrently and inextricably linguistic and behavioral. To give priority to either thoughts or actions at the theoretical level is to reproduce the prejudices of Cartesian ontology as well as the social division between mental and manual labor, which is typical of, though not exclusive to, industrial capitalism.[4]

The impetus to focus on linguistic phenomena in theorizing new directions in society comes not from a penchant for philosophical idealism but from transformations within the social system itself. In so many ways and in so many locations in the social landscape, action is mediated no longer mainly by speech but also by writing, a transformation long in the making, which has greatly accelerated in the past century.[5] With the development of large-scale organizations in every social sector except the family, written rules are codified in tracts and manuals, written records of transactions are preserved, and relationships are established and maintained by written documents. Literacy

[4]For a Marxist study of this distinction, see Alfred Sohn-Rethel, *Intellectual and Manual Labour: a Critique of Epistemology* (London: Macmillan, 1978).

[5]The history of writing and printing is a well-explored topic. I have found particularly useful Lucien Febvre and Henri-Jean Martin, *The Coming of the Book: the Impact of Printing, 1400–1800*, trans. David Gerard (London: Verso, 1984); and Elizabeth Eisenstein, *The Printing Press as an Agent of Change: Communications and Cultural Transformations in Early-Modern Europe* (New York: Cambridge University Press, 1979). The question of the influence of media on culture is also addressed by a position best represented by Marshall McLuhan, in which changes in media are related to changes in the balance of the sensorium. See Marshall McLuhan, *Understanding Media: The Extensions of Man* (New York: McGraw-Hill, 1964). Also of interest is Donald Lowe, *History of Bourgeois Perception* (Chicago: University of Chicago Press, 1982).

is not a cultural achievement but a means of survival in advanced societies. In addition to large-scale organizations, contemporary society has introduced discourse into practice by elaborating scientific methods. In the economy there are research teams and market surveys; in politics there are polls, censuses, and reports by commissions of trained researchers. It seems that nothing happens without first generating studies. In a society that requires expert opinion "scientific" research has attained an unprecedented prominence. When action is mediated not by speech but by writing a certain type of distance is introduced between individuals. The close connection between thoughts and speech, which had perhaps always been desired or even socially prescribed, rather than naturally existing,[6] is supplanted by the separation of thought and expression inherent in writing. With the spread of writing throughout society, the subject is structured in new ways and the question of the constitution of the subject in relation to modes of information is one of the main themes I plan to address.

The impact of writing on social relations is an old theme. Writing, after all, spread rapidly with the rise of capitalism.[7] The discussion of writing serves as a reminder of how language can change and as an introduction to my main theme —electronically mediated communication. For one can argue that the latter extends what had begun with the former: that electronically mediated communication intensifies the distance writing introduced between interacting individuals. The enormous temporal and spatial distances by which senders and receivers of written messages may be separated introduce the possibility for structural changes in language and in the way individuals are constituted by language.

Language is not simply a tool for expression; it is also a structure that defines the limits of communication and shapes the subjects who speak. Since Saussure, structuralists emphasize that language is a system that defines the subject. Mikhail Bakhtin adds that all linguistic phenomena are dialogic, part of an infinitely continuous web of communications whose meanings are not determined by the individual but are always open to redetermination by others. Austin continues the revision of the understanding of language by arguing that statements are not simply true or false but acts that do things to others. The

---

[6]See Jacques Derrida, *Of Grammatology*, trans. Gayatri Spivak (Baltimore: Johns Hopkins University Press, 1976), for an exploration of this theme.

[7]See Anthony Giddens's concept of time-space distanciation in *The Constitution of Society: Outline of the Theory of Structuration* (London: Polity, 1984).

gap between language and action is thus breached. Derrida contends that the internal separation within writing (*différance*) characterizes all experience. And Foucault takes perhaps the most radical stance by stepping completely outside the dualism of thought and action with his category discourse/practice. In these ways language has come to be seen as an enormously complicated phenomenon. It is not simply a vehicle of individual expression, a tool to facilitate action, a means to determine truths and falsehoods. It is instead an internally complex yet open world inextricably tied to social action.

The questions I am posing are these: What happens in society when the boundaries of linguistic experience are drastically transformed? How are social relations altered when language is no longer limited to face-to-face speech or to writing? What assumptions about the nature of society need to be revised when the already complex and ambiguous aspects of language are supplemented by electronic mediation?

Two theoretical temptations arise when these questions are posed, temptations that must be resisted because they lead to valid but limited strategies of inquiry. These possible lines of theorizing are technological determinism and linguistic formalism. Faced with a cluster of important recent technical innovations, some theorists have a tendency to interpret social change solely in relation to the invention, production, distribution, and use of new machines.[8] Televisions, video cassette recorders, computers, and satellite communications systems become, for them, the concrete substance of social reality. In this case, the social field is presumed to consist of material objects and human actions in relationship to them. The linguistic/symbolic level is obscured in such simple materialist analyses. All that some social scientists believe it necessary to know are the number of hours the television is on and the literal content of the programs. The only question posed here is what does the technology enable us to do? The material device is thought to be morally neutral.[9] And thus the machine is both isolated from its cultural context and invested with extraordinary powers. Instead of the age of the Reformation or the century of Louis XIV, we have the epoch of the Television or the Computer. While analyses that proceed from assumptions of technological determinism provide some interesting results, they also ig-

---

[8]See Larry Hirschhorn, *Beyond Mechanization: Work and Technology in a Postindustrial Age* (Cambridge: MIT Press, 1984).

[9]See Andrew Feenberg on the concept of technology in Marcuse in "The Bias of Technology," forthcoming.

nore important areas of inquiry and put aside the question of the emancipatory project of democratization.

At the other theoretical extreme from the technological determinists are the formalists. Here theory attempts to determine the valid model of communication in the new technological context. Mathematically based theories of information are an important direction of research. Language is reduced to units of significance and distinguished from noise. Quantitative formulas may then be devised to calculate the maximization of information over noise. From this standpoint, the new electronic communication devices benefit humankind since they increase the amount of information available to individuals as well as the number of information exchanges that take place in the social field. Other, very different formalists impose the model of poetry on the social field, concluding that the new electronic devices simply expand the volume of communicational garbage and provide no benefit at all. Between the mathematicians and the poets there are countless varieties of formalism, each of which takes some model of language as its discrete theoretical field and is concerned mainly with the internal attributes of that model.

The concept of the mode of information attempts to avoid the limitations of both the technological-determinist and the formalist approaches. It is designed to open as wide as possible a field of investigation into the changes in social relations that accompany the introduction of electronically mediated communication. It parallels the Marxist theory of the mode of production (hence the name) in that it presupposes that all communicationally based social relations are historically constituted and transitory; that the theorist has no epistemological ground upon which to stand to determine the universal, atemporal features of language; and finally that the aim of theory is to reveal the structures of domination as well as the liberatory potential in any given pattern of language experience.[10] The category of the mode of information is explicitly designed to aid the development of critical social theory.

But the concept of the mode of information departs from the prem-

[10]The character of domination and liberation with regard to patterns of language most centrally concern the cultural question of privileged forms of constituted subjects. As a form of domination, language (in its form, content, or context of enunciation) would confirm the white, male, middle-aged, heterosexual subject, for example, and configure other subjects in subordinated forms. The liberatory potential of a pattern of language consists in the manner in which it serves to undermine the dominant configuration of the subject.

ises of historical materialism in a number of fundamental ways. As a linguistically based theory, it rejects the priority given to labor in Marx's writings; labor continues to play a crucial role in societies with highly complex technologies, but the concept of labor is inadequate by itself to serve as the focus of the analysis of domination in these societies.

In addition, the theory of the mode of information eschews the teleological aspect of historical materialism. While one might admire the democratizing impulse that one finds, for instance, in Habermas's notion of communicative action, that impulse ought not be attached to an evolutionary design of history. Such a connection serves only to assist in the constitution of the object of inquiry as itself a structure of domination. If teleology were preserved in the theory of the mode of information, the linguistic element of the social field would become a "center" or an "essence" that would totalize the field and reduce all other aspects of the social field to it. Not only is this result politically disastrous from the perspective of the project of emancipation, as the history of the relation of socialism and feminism so disturbingly displays, but it is epistemologically unjustified, presuming as it does a privileged position for the theorist in which he or she might determine "objectively" or "in truth" the nature of the social whole.

The theory of the mode of information consciously plays itself against the theory of mode of production, seeking to undermine the theoretical hegemony of the latter if only to support its final purposes. At the most general level, the mode of production designates the way objects that satisfy human needs are made and exchanged. The mode of information designates the way symbols are used to communicate meanings and to constitute subjects. In the course of its usage, the mode of production came to be equated with society. Societies—in particular, capitalist society—were nothing more than modes of production. A society that contained, among other structures, a capitalist mode of production, appeared in Marxist discourse as simply "capitalist." The reductionist tendency in the mode of production must be avoided at all costs in the theory of the mode of information.

There is another, perhaps metaphorical sense, however, in which the mode of production was used to designate industrial societies. The mode of production in these societies attained a certain priority for social theory because industrial capitalism was a novelty and because it had a great impact on daily life. Thus one could think of industrial capitalist societies as "modes of production." The metaphorical use of the term *mode of production*, as distinct from its metonymic, reductionist use, can be transferred without undue risk to the term *mode of information*. Although every society contains a mode of information, contemporary societies with highly developed technologies are characterized by the emergence of a distinctly new mode of information, and the mode of information in these societies promises to alter the framework of social interactions radically. In that sense and in that sense alone, one may speak of these societies as modes of information, just as it was legitimate to speak of societies during the period of the rise and development of industrial capitalism as modes of production. But even in this usage it must be recalled that the term *mode of information* does not exhaust the meaning of the social field or the possible strategies of interpreting it. Rather it attempts analytically to isolate certain phenomena that may prove to be useful targets of investigation.

Within critical theory there have been several important efforts to elaborate a concept similar to the mode of information. Herbert Schiller shows how the capitalist elite controls the generation and dissemination of information, an important effort that reminds us not to forget the persistence of capitalist forms of ownership and control. Nonetheless, Schiller's work does not move in the direction of developing categories for the analysis of new communicational forms. Michel de Certeau employs a theory of narrative to analyze the resistance to dominant language codes in daily life. While such work is important it does not address the question of forms of linguistic experience that are peculiar to the twentieth century, and in particular the structures of domination they contain. Pierre Bourdieu has developed a paradigm for the analysis of everyday life which at once contains critical potential and effectively resists the reductive tendencies of historical materialism. In anthropology, Clifford Geertz's influential work proposes cultural analysis through the study of symbolic structures.[11]

[11]Herbert Schiller, *Who Knows: Information in the Age of the Fortune 500* (New York: Ablex, 1981); See Michel de Certeau, *The Practice of Everyday Life*, trans. Steven Rendall (Berkeley: University of California Press, 1984); Pierre Bourdieu, *La distinction: Critique sociale du jugement* (Paris: Minuit, 1979); and Bourdieu, *Language and Symbolic Power* (London: Polity, forthcoming); Clifford Geertz, *Interpretation of Cultures* (New York: Basic Books, 1973). For a more general orientation in this direction within social science, see Paul Rabinow and William M. Sullivan, *Interpretive Social Science: A Reader* (Berkeley: University of California Press, 1979).

Perhaps the most ambitious attempt to introduce the problem of language into critical social theory is the recent work by Jürgen Habermas. Habermas's idea of communicative rationality shifts the focus of critical theory from consciousness to language. But his work is rooted in the effort to define the nature of critical language usage (the ideal speech situation) more than the attempt to elaborate a framework for the empirical analysis of existing forms of linguistic experience.[12] Habermas is more intent on defining the linguistic origins of emancipatory action than he is in exploring the powerful new forms of linguistic "oppression" which have emerged in the past few decades. Television, computers, communication satellites are not often found in his texts. He continues the traditional philosophical (one might say metaphysical) project of determining the ontological foundation of a free society. Even though that ontological foundation is based in a schema of human development, which preserves the historical quality of the theory, it mistakenly attributes to the theorist the ability to define the universal attributes of the conditions of human speech.

Jean Baudrillard's work of the early 1970s is closer still to the project of the mode of information. In such works as *The Mirror of Production* and *Toward a Critique of the Political Economy of the Sign*, Baudrillard writes of "a mode of signification" in which Saussurean categories differentiate epochs of language forms. Since the Renaissance, Baudrillard contends, the sign has emerged as the dominant language form. He characterizes the sign as the increasing separation of signifier and signified. In the twentieth century the sign has been replaced by the signal. With the signal, words are structured to have reflexlike responses. Advertisements provide the best examples. The images they contain act as pure signifiers, divorced from any direct relation to the commodities they solicit. The consumer cannot raise the question of the relation of the word in the advertisement to the object it refers to. Instead, advertisements employ floating signifiers that merge with their newly defined referents, generating a signallike linguistic pattern. The standard linguistic process through which the recipient of the advertisement assimilates the message and responds with agreement or disagreement is short-circuited.[13] Sexual prowess (the sig-

---

[12]Jürgen Habermas, *The Theory of Communicative Action*, vol. 1: *Reason and the Rationalization of Society*, trans. Thomas McCarthy (Boston: Beacon, 1984).

[13]See Judith Williamson, *Decoding Advertisements: Ideology and Meaning in Advertising* (London: Marion Boyars, 1978), for examples of this process.

nifier) and an underarm deodorant (the object-referent) are merged into a communicational unit that works in linguistic practice like a stoplight.

The theory of the mode of signification is useful for the theory of mode of information, but it is limited by its formalist assumptions. Working only with Saussurean categories, Baudrillard reached an impasse with his concept of the code—that which structures and gives meaning to signals. Communication is reduced to an all-encompassing code through which the semiological field is totalized. Escape from the code is possible only at the margins: in death, in graffiti, in the passive-aggressive strategy of seduction. In addition to this limitation, Baudrillard's work opens an analytic field only at the level of semiology. It does not lend itself to the study of linguistic phenomena beyond those associated with the marketing and distribution of commodities, such as the techniques of surveillance or the communicational abilities of computers. As a regional analysis of the linguistic structure of advertising and commodities, however, Baudrillard's work remains important.

The theory of the mode of information proceeds from the modest assumption that no one set of categories is adequate to analyze the varied new forms of communicational experiences. The mode of information, therefore, is to be thought of not as a unified field but as a multiplicity of discourses/practices, each requiring its own categories of analysis. For example, the recipient of the message is structured differently in each discourse/practice. In the cases of television commercials, working at a computer, and surveillance, the individual receives messages from the electronic machine but is structured in relation to that machine in very different ways.

The television commercial structures the desire of a consumer and constitutes that consumer abstractly and generally. In the process of producing the advertisement, consumers are sampled for their response to different versions and various aspects of it. Careful studies are done to determine the most advantageous presentation of the product. The advertiser aims for the widest possible target group. Commercials for expensive commodities ignore less affluent groups, for example. Thus, commercials are structured to appeal to a group; yet they are usually experienced by an isolated individual who is viewing television or listening to radio. The message of the advertisement must disguise the disparity that it is carefully structured in relation to its recipient but that the recipient is a generalized other who is constituted by the ad.

The nineteenth-century novel provides a striking contrast to the television commercial. The novel was also communicated to many people in individual experiences, but the novelist did not meticulously study his or her potential audience or minutely construct the work to create a positive impression on the reader. The novelist was certainly aware of the culture of the potential audience and was just as certainly shaping the novel to produce an effect on the imagination of the reader and, in that sense, resembled the advertiser. The purchase of a product was also at stake, in this case the book itself. The commodity aspect of the novel was also prominent in serial novels of the nineteenth century, whose dramatic structure was shaped by the need to heighten the reader's attention so that the next installment would be purchased.[14] In fact, some twentieth-century novels, such as the Harlequin romances, have been influenced by the techniques of advertising. These formula books are aimed at a generalized other who is treated, in the shaping of the book, like a consumer.[15] But the nineteenth-century novel differed from the television commercial in the crucial respect that it constructed the recipient of the communication in relation to the constraints of a relatively coherent bourgeois culture, whereas the advertisement does so within a postmodern mass culture composed of decontextualized images and signs, of floating signifiers and designer language.

The mode of information of the television commercial as it pertains to the recipient of the message requires such semiological categories as the floating signifier for analysis. The analysis of the communicational phenomena of surveillance employs different analytical categories. Surveillance is itself a many-sided phenomenon. It includes everything from the gathering of information about particular individuals by governmental organizations such as the Federal Bureau of Investigation to, at the other extreme, the routine accumulation of information about anonymous citizens that occurs automatically when long-distance phone calls are made, when credit cards are used, when

[14]On serial novels, see Lewis Coser's chapter "The Commercialization of Writing" in *Men of Ideas: A Sociologist's View* (New York: Free Press, 1965).
[15]For an analysis of romance novels, see Leslie Rabine, *Reading the Romantic Heroine: Text, History, Ideology* (Ann Arbor: University of Michigan Press, 1985).

books are borrowed from libraries, and so forth. In this chapter I restrict the discussion of surveillance to the latter group of cases. The memory capacity of computers enables the monitoring of the activity of vast segments of the population. When an individual uses a credit card, he or she sends to various agencies a message that is "remembered," filed, and integrated with other messages. The collection of such messages constitutes a data base, which then serves a monitoring function with regard to the individual who originally made the credit card purchase. At any time thereafter agencies may exchange communications that include, directly or indirectly, information about the original transaction. In this way, the individual is "spoken" about in the communication between memory banks of agencies, without knowing anything about the "conversation." In addition, these communications may have direct consequence to the individual if, for example, he or she is applying for a loan or planning a revolution.

In the case of computer monitoring the individual is the recipient of a message (when he or she applies for a loan, when his or her insurance rates go up, or when his or her local community enacts an ordinance limiting certain literature in libraries after a study is made of library use). This message is often "received" in a most indirect manner, even though it may have an important impact on the individual's life. The message is also a "response" to a message from that individual, since it is composed to reflect information a tiny part of which is the inadvertent message the individual "sent" when he or she made a purchase by credit card, for example. In the case of surveillance, the issue for the mode of information is less the constitution of the subject as a consumer (as in the television commercial) than the political control of the individual by computer monitoring.

The individual is politically controlled because decisions are made (about him or her individually or about the local or national community) in which the individual has lost the power to respond directly. Let us be clear about what is at stake in surveillance. The individual participated in a social interaction and unintentionally left behind a trace communication. That communication was collected by an agency. Subsequently, that agency or another agency carried out an action that affected the individual. Now it is true that individuals always leave traces of their actions (the person who made the sale might remember something about the consumer), and these traces might have a later influence on the individual (the salesperson might testify in a case concerning the individual but having nothing to do with the sale). The computer, however, permits the systematic collection of this data and its infinite transferability in time and space (the salesperson would be unlikely to be interviewed by a loan-granting agency years later about the character of the individual). The difference between casual and computer memory is crucial, for it constitutes the basis for systematic surveillance. With computer monitoring the individual is the "recipient" of messages of control, a process that has been generalized to the point that, under the mode of information, all individuals have become aware of "receiving" this message; that is, they are aware that their lives are constantly being monitored in matters that are "private" and in ways that are beyond their ken.

In the mode of information, the recipient of a message is structured still differently in the case of the use of a computer by an individual. Neither semiological nor political categories are of much use in this set of cases. Indeed, the analysis of the communication structure of the use of a computer involves philosophical issues about the nature of the mind and the subject.[16] For the computer is a new kind of reality, neither completely like the mind nor completely like matter. It is a borderline phenomenon, bringing into question the limit of the substances on each side of line.[17] On the one hand, the computer is simply a machine, a combination, however complex, of natural materials refashioned by human beings. On the other hand, the computer has several qualities that are like those of the mind, as proponents of artificial intelligence remind us.[18] Typing on the computer keyboard is similar to using a typewriter. Keys are stroked, and material traces result. But with the computer these traces are instantaneously manipulable; they lack the inertia of ink on paper. Figures on a monitor come and go as quickly as thoughts in the mind. Writing on a computer is something like speaking, in the sense that corrections are made immediately; there is no rubbing out, removing from matter what one has placed there. And yet of course that does occur in the computer.

[16]See Jean Zeitoun, "Codes et langages pour un sujet terminal," *Travers/26* (October 1982), 72–79.
[17]Sherry Turkle explores this theme in psychological terms in *The Second Self: Computers and the Human Spirit* (New York: Simon and Schuster, 1984), p. 31.
[18]For a statement of the position against artificial intelligence, see Hubert Dreyfus, *What Computers Can't Do: A Critique of Artificial Reason* (New York: Harper and Row, 1972); and more recently *Mind over Machine: The Power of Human Intuition and Expertise in the Era of the Computer* (New York: Free Press, 1986).

Minute traces are placed and removed from memory or from the metal oxide film on the disk.

The computer creates a communicational situation for the subject in which the subject's distinctive traits are put into question. The subject finds itself confronting a machine that mimics its qualities and in some respects (memory, calculations) transcends its abilities. When the computer is connected through telephone lines to other computers, the situation becomes even more complex. The subject can then access the memory banks of remote computers, can send messages to groups of individuals at the same time, or can have ongoing "conversations" with people through their computers.[19] In each of these instances, the individual using a computer is in a new linguistic situation.

In traditional Cartesian terms, the subject is a mind that confronts material objects or other minds. The subject is constituted as a thinking thing confronting a fixed world. With the computer these Cartesian presuppositions, which in many ways are characteristic of the dominant culture in the modern world, are seriously destabilized.[20] The subject now includes objects that perhaps do not think (if thinking requires a conscious I),[21] but that do things that resemble aspects of thinking and outperform thinking subjects in ways that are important to them. For example, in the Cartesian world, only individual minds have knowledge; the rest of nature is dumb. Now, however, when the subject has access to a data base he or she is confronted by a machine that *appears* to "know" more than the subject. In a sense, the data base is no more than a library, a material world of mental traces. But the speed with which the data is available to the subject in the computerized data base changes the subject's experience. Getting information from the data base is more like speaking to another, very erudite subject than like using the library where the subject's body must be dragged through space to locate information.

At the ontological level metaphysical dualists may argue that nothing has changed with the introduction of computer. The world may still be thought by some to be composed of material and mental things.

[19]See Starr Roxanne Hiltz and Murray Turoff, *The Network Nation: Human Communication via Computer* (London: Addison-Wesley, 1978).

[20]For an elaboration of the relation of Descartes and modernity, see Michel Foucault, *Histoire de la folie* (Paris: Plon, 1961). Also useful in this regard is Richard Rorty, *Philosophy and the Mirror of Nature* (Princeton: Princeton University Press, 1979).

[21]See A. M. Turing, "Computing Machinery and Intelligence," *Mind* 59 (October 1950), 433–60. This essay put the controversy over artificial intelligence on a new level.

But at the phenomenological level at which the subject experiences itself and the world, the computer changes everything. The subject finds itself in relations with computers, ambiguous objects that refute in practice the Cartesian dualist world, that do not act like objects, that therefore call into question the nature of the subjectivity of the subject. Like the other domains of the mode of information, the computer draws attention to the subject as a constituted phenomenon, undermining the illusory assurance of the fixed, defined individual. The computer, like the television ad and the system of surveillance, brings to the fore the fact that individuals are constituted subjects and in so doing reconstitutes subjects as subjects that are always already constituted, never naturally given. The mode of information marks a new epoch in that in it the process of the subject's self-constitution becomes the discourse/practice of communication in everyday life. Linguistic experience in the mode of information is *about self-constitution*, whereas in earlier epochs that process was at best only implicit, disguised by a thousand ideological veils, including the idea of human nature; the doctrine of the immortality of the soul; the sense of having a fixed personality, which arises from experiencing daily only those people in the small world of one's birth; the fiction that there is a truth about oneself revealed in the confessional; the pretense that the therapeutic session reenacts the drama of the formation of one's personality, which derives, ultimately, from a family romance; the ancient Greek discourse/practice of the art of living for noblemen only.

Although these examples demonstrate the multiplicity of discourses within the mode of information, there remains a more general level in which the mode of information is unified, not segmented. The mode of information coheres as a unity in four respects: (1) all its parts concern communications, (2) all are mediated by electronic mechanisms, (3) all point to the self as constructed or constituted, rather than as a stable, centered entity, and (4) the goal of the investigation is the discovery of structures of domination. While these unifying elements are important, the decisive moment of analysis, especially at this early stage of my investigation, remains the more concrete level of regional investigation. Problems of hasty conceptual closure which are introduced by interpretive strategies that rely upon totalizing and reductionist figures are held at bay when discontinuous multiplicity is built into the theoretical infrastructure.[22] If each region of investigation is

---

[22]See Jean-François Lyotard's notion of phrases in *Le différend* (Paris: Gallimard, 1984).

theorized with its unique conceptual apparatus, the mode of information emerges as a patched quilt, rather than as whole cloth. Concepts that open an effective hermeneutic on the question of surveillance will not work to decode advertisements or to reveal the new epistemology of using a computer. The structures of domination within the mode of information will thus be grasped as distinct "technologies of power," to use Foucault's apt phrase. And the theory itself will be relatively free of the elements of domination that are typically found in totalizing positions.

One dimension of the theory of the mode of information which requires further development is the question of historical periodicity. My assumption is that earlier social formations contained modes of information and that these were different from that of the twentieth century. I use the generic term *mode of information* in relation to the current form of the mode of information only to underscore its importance and novelty in the present. A more adequate formulation might be "the *electronic* mode of information," but for the time being I want to avoid this term for two reasons: (1) the qualifier has a totalizing implication and must be carefully delimited; (2) without determining the earlier incarnations of the mode of information the best term for its current form cannot be decided.

One promising initial line of investigation into the mode of information is Foucault's problematic of the constitution of the self. Foucault developed this theoretical strategy as an alternative to phenomenological positions on the self as consciousness and to structuralist occlusions of the self as an object of analysis. His position is that the subject is neither fixed (as in phenomenology) nor marginal (as in structuralism). In order to assess the value of Foucault's contribution, it is necessary to comprehend the context of the controversy between phenomenologists and structuralists. The important issue at stake in the debate is perhaps the leading theme or metanarrative of Western thought since the Enlightenment, individualism.

Individualism, or the rational self, has been a central preoccupation of Western writing for the past 250 years. It became prominent in the context of the formation of capitalist, modern society, although that context was not always explicitly thematized by writers. The notion that the individual is a unity and that the unity is grounded in a capacity for autonomous thought has had a remarkably compelling attraction for writers. Phenomenologists such as Edmund Husserl and existentialists such as Sartre shifted the ground of unity from rationality to consciousness, a broader and perhaps more flexible term. Structuralists, in response, postulated a transindividual level of meaning, centered in language or society depending on the writer's commitments, but neither alternative was entirely satisfactory. Neither could account for the other's object of analysis, and each totalized its position in a way that excluded the other's object of analysis.

Foucault had been working with a concept of detotalized discourse/practice which went a long way toward overcoming the theoretical limitations of the dualisms associated with the theory of the rational individual. The notion that society is a fragmented multiplicity of discourses/practices is an excellent corrective to many of the impasses of social theory, but it does not address the issue of the individual. Foucault developed the problematic of the constitution of the self precisely to account for the individual without resorting to rationalist, phenomenological, or structuralist assumptions. The individual was now theorized as a process in which the self was constituted through the mediation of discourses/practices. The individual in this view is neither an ontological center nor a passive, marginal "bearer" of other levels of analysis. The attraction of Foucault's position is that it authorizes the analysis of the individual without ontologizing it, centering it, or marginalizing it. It allows the historical analysis of the self without privileging any one definition of the self. Moreover it removes the interpretive question of validity from the level of theory and places it where it should be, at the level of concrete analysis. Whether or not a particular study of the constitution of the self is "correct" depends not on the theoretical framework of the study but on the final presentation of the analysis itself, an analysis that can only achieve a status of validity from the community of readers. The question of truth is thus shifted from the ontological level to the historicoempirical level, at once undermining the metaphysical power of the author and the cultural prejudice of rational individualism.

Foucault left off his analysis at the crucial point of the mid–twentieth century. He never went beyond Freudian psychoanalysis as a discourse/practice in which the self was constituted. As a consequence his position suffered from a lack of historical rootedness: his approach was well situated in relation to other positions, but its own importance and direction was left undefined.[23] This deficiency can be considerably

---

[23]Foucault wrestles with this problem in "What Is Enlightenment?" trans. Catherine Porter, in Paul Rabinow, ed., *The Foucault Reader* (New York: Pantheon, 1984).

reduced by placing the problematic of the constitution of the self in relation to the mode of information. The analysis then moves from discourses/practices that are limited to such phenomena as the Christian confessional and the psychoanalytic session to the more extensive arena of electronically mediated communication.

8

The Family and the
Mode of Information

The many difficulties faced by the contemporary family have brought forth some highly pessimistic prognoses. One of them, the hypothesis offered by Christopher Lasch to explain the situation of the family today, has received considerable recognition and deserves our attention. In a series of highly regarded but controversial books, Lasch argues that the nuclear family is disappearing, though he arrives at his conclusion without empirically investigating any families.[1] Instead, he reviews a variety of cultural phenomena in search of what they reveal about the moral stature of Americans. He contends that the nuclear family nurtured strong egos and superegos as a consequence of unambiguous paternal domination. With fathers clearly in charge of the family and mothers specializing in the care of their young, children confronted firm and repressive discipline, a pattern that I call the exchange of parental love for bodily gratification.[2]

Lasch warns that today's family no longer inculcates strong egos, one of the bases for democracy, or strong superegos, the foundation for personal self-restraint. He recites a litany of modern family trends

---

[1]See Christopher Lasch, *Haven in a Heartless World: The Family Besieged* (New York: Basic, 1977); *The Culture of Narcissism: American Life in an Age of Diminishing Expectations* (New York: Norton, 1979); and *The Minimal Self: Psychic Survival in Troubled Times* (New York: Norton, 1984). For a recent study of the question of narcissism, see Fred Alford, *Narcissism: Socrates, the Frankfurt School, and Psychoanalytic Theory* (New Haven: Yale University Press, 1988).

[2]See Mark Poster, *Critical Theory of the Family* (New York: Continuum, 1978).

responsible, he says, for the narcissism rampant in our culture: "the emergence of the egalitarian family, so-called; the child's increasing exposure to other socializing agencies besides the family; and the general effect of modern mass culture in breaking down distinctions between illusions and reality." "The modern family," Lasch maintains, "is the product of egalitarian ideology, consumer capitalism and therapeutic intervention." Child care outside the family "expose[s] children to new forms of manipulation, sexual seduction, and outright sexual exploitation." Children watch too much television, attend too many child-care centers, eat junk food, "listen to junk music, read junk comics and spend endless hours playing video games, because their parents are too busy or too harried to offer them proper nourishment for their minds and bodies. They attend third-rate schools and get third-rate advice from their elders." Finally, "many children today encounter less and less cultural opposition to fantasies of sexual and generational interchangeability," which are strengthened by "early exposure to sexual images," by sex education, and by the idea of children's equality with adults.[3]

The core of Lasch's argument is taken from psychoanalysis: the hysterical patients of Freud's time have been replaced today by narcissists, individuals who are unable to define the boundaries of their own egos, who merge self and other, thereby confusing their own gratification with their relations with others.[4] Heinz Kohut, a psychoanalyst whose writing Lasch relies upon heavily, describes the change this way: "During the era preceding our own, the overstimulating closeness with the adults to which the child was exposed led later in adult life to the hostilities and inhibitions which . . . Freud's explanations may have ultimately helped us to overcome to a degree. Now we may see the results of a deadening distance to which children are exposed, leading in adulthood to a different kind of psychopathology, the disorders of the self."[5] If nineteenth-century hysterics were symp-

---

[3]Lasch, *Minimal Self*, pp. 185, 186, 188–89, 191. Extrafamilial influences on the family have been observed by many other social scientists. An early proponent of this position is Alexander Mitscherlich, an associate of the Frankfurt School, in *Society without the Father*, trans. Eric Mosbacher (New York: Schocken, 1963).

[4]Lasch uses the term *narcissism* in several ways, somewhat diminishing its analytic power in his text. For an excellent critique of his use of the term, see Jesse Battan, "The 'New Narcissism' in 20th-Century America: The Shadow and Substance of Social Change," *Journal of Social History* 17.2 (1978), 199–220. Battan concludes that "the concept of narcissism merely clouds our understanding of . . . complex social and cultural issues" (p. 221).

[5]Heinz Kohut, "Thoughts on Narcissism and Narcissistic Rage (1972)," in *Self Psychol-*

tomatic of the oedipal family in being incapable of repressing their urges as the family trained them to do, contemporary narcissists bespeak a different family pattern, in which parents do not deeply care about their children and make little effort to define limits to the child's experience, in which, in default of parental attention, children are left at the mercy of "dangerous" nonfamily institutions—child-care centers, commercial television, the helping professions. Instead of being subject to a clear repression of bodily gratification, the child is indulged so as not to demand much attention. Lasch contends that in this family context the child's fantasies run wild, stimulated by urges it neither controls nor comprehends. The child's ego remains weak, since it has little sense of achieving mastery over its body, and its superego indistinct, since it has not clearly internalized definite parental images.

In therapy sessions, Lasch reports, narcissistic patients "regularly describe their fathers as 'ciphers' while characterizing their mothers as both seductive and 'mortally dangerous.'" The father's emotional absence removes, for these individuals, "an important obstacle to the child's illusion of omnipotence." Today the threat of nuclear destruction heightens these family tendencies. People want to take their pleasures without thinking of tomorrow. Within the family, the fear of imminent destruction intensifies the fear of separation and "weakens the psychological resources that make it possible to confront this fear realistically." In addition, Lasch continues, society contributes to narcissism by substituting a consumerist fantasy world of objects for a real world that might be controlled and mastered. In the haze of electronically transmitted images, individuals fuse their own dreams with the fantasies they imbibe from the culture, further confounding the border between self and other.[6]

Lasch's denunciation of the practices of the contemporary family is powerful and coherent. My research on the middle-class family in Orange County, California, indicates, however, that it is largely mistaken, at least with regard to this group. Lasch's pronouncement is too sweeping in its claims, generalizing too easily from psychoanalytic diagnoses of narcissism to sociological conditions; it overlooks many of the advances in contemporary families over the limitations of the oedipal family (limitations Lasch does not acknowledge); and it fails to

---

ogy and the Humanities: Reflections on a New Psychoanalytic Approach, ed. Charles Strozier (New York: Norton, 1985), p. 168.
   [6]Lasch, *The Minimal Self*, p. 191.

distinguish excesses in cultural patterns, which may be harmful to individuals, from the cultural patterns themselves, which may offer new possibilities for genuine gratification.

To test the thesis of narcissism, I asked Orange County mothers to describe how they reacted to the "terrible two" phase of their child's development. Parents who engender narcissistic tendencies confuse their own feelings with those of their child's, being unclear about the boundary of their egos.[7] About one-third responded in ways indicating that narcissism might be a problem: they believed their children during the terrible twos are testing their parents' wills or challenging their authority. Half the mothers think their children are attempting to define their own boundaries by the behavior, a clear indication of a sense of separateness of parent and child. The remaining group is divided between those who respond to the child in an authoritarian manner by answering that they think the child is asking for discipline, and those who have a somewhat conventional attitude, stating simply that the child is going through a phase.

In another question I attempt to detect the degree of the mother's anxiety when she is separated from the child, a possible sign of a desire for merger with the child or of a need for total control of the child. Mothers were asked if they feared the child would break things if not constantly watched. About 7 percent indicated that they are often beset by this fear. Another 28 percent said "sometimes." Those in the first group may tend to hover over the child, restricting his or her ability to achieve autonomy and perhaps developing narcissistic tendencies. Overall, however, very few mothers demonstrate narcissogenic tendencies, either by confusing self boundaries or by evincing a lack of concern for their children.[8] More work needs to be done to reach firm conclusions on this question, work that examines families more intensively than is possible using survey research methods.

If there are no clear indications of parental boundary confusion and narcissism in my findings, Lasch's other intuition, that there is a new

---

[7]In an excellent article on the question of the historical roots of narcissism, see Michael Bader and Ilene Philipson, "Narcissism and Family Structure: A Social-Historical Perspective," *Psychoanalysis and Contemporary Thought* 3.3 (1980), 299–328. They define narcissism as "the incapacity to hold oneself in esteem as an autonomous being and to wholly love and be intimate with another [which derives from] the difficulty in an earlier period of self-other differentiation vis-à-vis the mother" (p. 311).

[8]One would not expect people who fill out questionnaires on the family to be indifferent to their children. On this count no conclusion can be reached about narcissism based on a self-selecting sample.

pattern in family life, is confirmed. Three-quarters of the mothers work outside the homes. More than 85 percent send their children to day-care centers or preschools. Almost all have televisions; one-quarter have three or more; three-quarters own video cassette recorders. Most spouse/partners participate to some extent in child care, housecleaning, and cooking, domains that nineteenth-century patriarchs scrupulously shirked. Orange County families are, in Lasch's terms, "egalitarian," prey to "consumer capitalism," and they freely subject their children to the "dangers" of child-care centers.

Yet if Lasch's diagnosis of narcissism is largely incorrect, psychoanalysis itself may be in question. Perhaps the Freudian categories concerning the first three libidinal phases and the Oedipus complex itself are no longer germane to understanding family emotional processes. Perhaps Foucault was right in his critique of Freud in volume 1 of *The History of Sexuality* when he reconstructed psychoanalysis as a discourse/practice that constituted an oedipal configuration of the family rather than providing a point of departure for its analysis.[9] To pursue these theoretical questions I want to ask what new family patterns have emerged to replace the oedipal family and how families are shaped by the mode of information.

There are, no doubt, serious methodological differences between the earlier chapters of this book, which rely on critical theory and poststructuralism, and this one, which relies upon a positivist research instrument, a questionnaire I used for a research project begun in 1986. Foucault's work might more properly suggest an analysis of magazines and books that advise parents and portray ideal family practices. Instead, I chose the survey method because I felt a need, rightly or wrongly, for direct evidence of family life, echoing the work of Adorno and the Frankfurt School on the psychology of fascism and achieving perhaps the same mixed results they obtained.[10]

To obtain a sample of families, I distributed invitations to participate in the study through preschools, day-care centers, and kindergarten classes in public schools in Irvine, Laguna Beach, Newport Beach, and

---

[9]Michel Foucault, *The History of Sexuality*, vol. 1: *An Introduction*, trans. Robert Hurley (New York: Pantheon, 1978). A similar critique of Freud can be found in the work of Gilles Deleuze and Félix Guattari. See *Anti-Oedipus: Capitalism and Schizophrenia*, trans. Robert Hurley et al. (Minneapolis: University of Minnesota Press, 1983); and Deleuze and Guattari, *A Thousand Plateaus: Capitalism and Schizophrenia*, trans. Brian Massumi (Minneapolis: University of Minnesota Press, 1987).

[10]Theodor Adorno et al., *The Authoritarian Personality* (New York: Norton, 1969).

El Toro—all cities in Orange County, California. I selected preschools randomly from the phone directory. The Irvine School District (the only public school in the sample) was selected because of its location in a largely middle-class community. Only families with at least one child age six or younger were invited, so that parents had been involved with feeding, toilet training, and sexuality relatively recently. Families that responded to the invitation were mailed questionnaires. These asked that mothers fill them out and return them by mail.[11] If after two weeks the questionnaires were not returned, mothers were contacted by phone and reminded about them. Approximately three thousand invitations were distributed, eliciting 318 responses; 290 mothers returned completed questionnaires. I drew up the questions based on my knowledge of the oedipal family. Most were closed-end questions with a response scale graded 1 to 5, from strongly agree to strongly disagree.[12]

The respondents to my questionnaire are by no means representative of the population of Orange County, much less the United States. I distributed the instrument in some of the wealthier communities in the southern part of the county because I wanted to compare a more affluent group today to the nineteenth-century group that was most similar to the oedipal or classical nuclear family. By this means I could measure the endurance of the nuclear family in the social class associated with its birth and early development. It is possible that the oedipal family remains characteristic of Orange County even if it is not prevalent in the social group I studied. It is known that for certain indicators, particularly sexual attitudes, the contemporary working-class family more closely resembles the classical nuclear family than does the contemporary middle class.[13]

Because I distributed the questionnaire only to households with children it is not surprising to learn that they were somewhat larger in

[11]I requested that "mothers" complete the questionnaire to avoid inconsistency of informants. By designating the "mother" rather than say the "female adult" I allowed for male adults who consider themselves "mothers" to participate in the study. If a family contained two partners and both considered themselves mothers, both would answer the questionnaire.

[12]Open-ended questions that were coded and included in the study concerned (1) the occupation of the respondent and spouse/partner, and (2) books and magazines consulted by the respondent on child-care issues. A copy of the questionnaire can be obtained by writing to Professor Mark Poster, History Department, University of California, Irvine, Irvine, Calif., 92717.

[13]See Jeffrey Weeks, *Sex, Politics and Society: The Regulation of Sexuality Since 1800* (London: Longman, 1981).

Table 1. Size of household

Number of people	Frequency	Percentage
2	18	6.2
3	75	25.9
4	130	44.8
5	42	14.5
6	14	4.8
7	7	2.4
8 or more	4	1.4
Total	290	100.0

Table 2. Family income

Income	Frequency	Percentage
Less than $20,000	20	7.0
$20,000 to 35,000	36	12.7
$35,000 to 50,000	68	24.0
$50,000 to 65,000	53	18.7
More than $65,000	106	37.5
Total	283	99.9

size than the average American household. The average household among the respondents was 4, somewhat above the national figure (see Table 1).[14] The family income of the participants in the study was very high (see Table 2), reflecting the occupations of the respondents. Among both the men and the women who worked, there were disproportionately high numbers of professionals, managers, and proprietors. Only a handful listed working-class, service, or white-collar occupations associated with lower salaries. A few students accounted for most of the families with incomes under $20,000. Nearly all the respondents were female; only 5 of 290 were male. Nearly all (92 percent) were white. The next largest racial group was Asians, only 3.5 percent of the total, a distribution not uncommon in the cities surveyed.

The religious preference of the respondents is not untypical of the class and the location of the sample (see Table 3).[15] Even though about

[14]The national figure for 1984 is an astonishing 2.71. This figure is down from 4.76 in 1900 and 5.79 in 1790, the earliest record. See *Household and Family Characteristics, March 1984* (Washington, D.C.: Bureau of the Census, 1985), p. 9.

[15]See *Statistical Abstracts of the U.S.* (Washington, D.C.: Bureau of the Census, 1986).

Table 3. Religious preference

Religion	Frequency	Percentage
Catholic	49	18.6
Jewish	23	8.7
Mormon	13	4.9
Protestant	99	37.5
Other	30	11.4
No preference	50	18.9
Total	264	100.0

Table 4. Age of respondents

Age	Frequency	Percentage
20 to 29 years	66	22.8
30 to 39 years	201	70.3
Over 39 years	21	6.9
Total	288	100.0

10 percent of the invitations to participate in the study were distributed to families with children in denominational preschools, the respondents were disproportionately nonreligious. One-third never attended a worship center; another 28 percent attended only a few times a year. Only 27 percent attended church at least once a week.

The group was older than might be expected. Since I am most interested in the early years of child rearing, I wanted families with young children. Yet most of the respondents were between thirty and thirty-nine (see Table 4). Only about one-quarter were twenty-nine or younger, the youngest being twenty. These figures support the picture of a national trend in which women bear children later in the life cycle.[16]

With regard to marital status, an index important to my study, the group was highly uncharacteristic both of Orange County and of the nation, for 86 percent of the respondents were married, two-thirds of them for the first time. Fewer than 3 percent had never been married. Clearly, in this respect the group under study is very much like the classical nuclear family. The ideal of the oedipal family was lifelong

[16]See Prithwis Das Gupta, *Future Fertility of Women by Present Age and Parity: Analysis of American Historical Data, 1917–80* (Washington, D.C.: Bureau of the Census, 1985), p. 3.

Table 5. Years living with spouse/partner

Number of years	Frequency	Percentage
Less than 3	7	2.9
3 to 5	26	10.7
6 to 10	88	36.4
More than 10	121	50.0
Total	242	100.0

association, and there were very few divorces in the nineteenth century; marriages were broken mainly by death of one partner. In addition, the respondents are unusual for Orange County in that they have been together for a long time (see Table 5). Over 86 percent had been with their current spouse/partner more than five years, and half for more than ten years. The families under review were thus unusually committed to their marriages. In this respect as well they resembled their nineteenth-century counterparts. The only reason for the unrepresentative marital stability of the participants I can offer is that participation is somehow related to the conformity of the family to the dominant ideal about "good" families.

On many important criteria, then, this group closely resembled the late nineteenth-century nuclear family: they were white; they had few children; they were married, largely for the first time; and they had been together for a long time. If these families' emotional structure varied considerably from the oedipal family, it would be strong evidence that the classical nuclear family has disappeared from the group in which it originated and therefore may in general be on the wane.

One other important variable in the profile of the families studied needs to be discussed: the respondents' occupations. One-quarter of the respondents listed their occupation as housewife. In the nineteenth century this figure would have been over 99 percent. By contrast with the mothers of the past, many women now work outside the home. In this respect the designation "nuclear family," as sociologists have shown, applies to only 10 percent of the population in the United States.[17] This change in women's job status is one of the most profound social trends affecting the family and is no doubt an important condition for many of the other changes in the family which I have observed.

[17]Marvin Harris, "Growing Conservatism? Not in Family Patterns," *Los Angeles Times,* December 23, 1981, pt. II, p. 9.

One of the main findings of my study is that the child-rearing patterns of the classical nuclear family have been almost completely abandoned. The contemporary Orange County child confronts a structure of authority and love different from the one faced by his or her nineteenth century counterpart. If the nuclear family can be understood in part as a pattern in which the child, during the early years, receives parental affection in exchange for relinquishing bodily gratification, then the nuclear family no longer exists. In what follows I document these changes and then present such portraits of the new family structures as my sample permits.

In the nineteenth century scheduled breast feeding was the norm for the middle class. In my study only 5 percent of mothers breast-fed, and of these, only two, or 15 percent, scheduled the feeding. Bottle feeding, the alternative adopted by the majority of mothers, offers advantages that are apparently highly valued in today's families. Bottle feeding enables spouses/partners to share in the feeding activity. More than 77 percent of those using bottle feeding stated that their spouse/partner shared the activity to some extent. In this regard, middle-class families in Orange County have overwhelmingly rejected the strict sex-role segregation of their nineteenth-century counterparts. A mere 16 percent, however, share the feeding activity equally. Already something of a pattern in child rearing is emerging: while the strict division of tasks between man and woman has been rejected, the redistribution of child rearing has been moderate, perhaps indicating that although the man's privileged role in the family has been rejected in principle, the practice of sex-defined tasks has not been radically altered.

Again rejecting the nineteenth-century pattern, the few schedule feeders prefer flexibility to rigid adherence to the clock. The nineteenth-century ideal of machinelike regularity in feeding has been abandoned. The child's bodily needs now take priority over what was once the regimen of industrial punctuality. In addition only 10 percent nurse longer than one year, whereas in the classical nuclear family, in part under the influence of Jean-Jacques Rousseau and the romantic movement, extended breast feeding by mothers was the norm. Among breast feeders a potential fear is insufficient milk, but fewer than a fourth of the breast-feeding mothers reported they experienced such anxiety, an indication that the mothers are well nourished, and also a sign that the feeding is accomplished with confidence. Almost 90 percent said that feeding was a happy, relaxed experience for them.

There is some evidence that in the nineteenth century middle-class mothers were insecure about breast feeding, burdened as the activity was with high moral and spiritual purposes.[18] Such insecurity corresponds with their imposition of a rigid schedule. It bespeaks a circumstance in which mothers were breaking with the tradition of employing wet nurses as well as their newfound isolation from older women's networks in the privacy of the nuclear family.[19] The relative absence of such anxiety today suggests an emotionally fuller experience for both parent and infant, whether it is being fed by its mother or her spouse/partner. It might be mentioned that the perception of feeding as sometimes being a chore was proportionally about equally distributed among sampled Orange County mothers between the housewives and mothers who work outside the home (about one-third for each group), a finding that contradicts the view that working mothers are less able to enjoy child rearing than housewives.

These observations lead to the issue of the degree of isolation of the family both from relatives and from the community. More than 40 percent of the mothers never got advice from a relative about feeding, and almost 60 percent never got advice from a friend. Of those who did get advice on feeding from a relative, three-fourths got it from their mothers. Mothers in the sample turned more frequently to doctors and to literature. Of the 80 percent who received advice on feeding from doctors, one-half thought the advice important. Only one-fourth of the mothers consulted other health-care professionals on the subject, but the vast majority read books and magazines on feeding. Of these, two-thirds named *Parents Magazine* as the periodical of choice, and Dr. Benjamin Spock was the author most frequently mentioned. It is worth noting that the mothers' attitudes about child rearing closely resembled those of Dr. Spock, just as those of nineteenth-century middle-class mothers tended to follow contemporary medical opinion.

These results imply that parents today are considerably isolated from kin and community. Since Orange County is a rapidly growing area with a population of one million in 1965, which doubled by 1980, many residents have emigrated from elsewhere, leaving relatives and friends behind. Daily life in suburban Orange County, with its cen-

[18]Mary Ryan, *Womanhood in America* (New York: Watts, 1983), p. 144.
[19]Carroll Smith-Rosenberg, in "The Female World of Love and Ritual: Relations between Women in Nineteenth-Century America," in *Disorderly Conduct: Visions of Gender in Victorian America* (New York: Oxford, 1985), pp. 53–76, shows how some women's networks survived the privacy of the nuclear family.

tralized shopping malls and few places for casual congregation, discourages the formation of new ties. There is little evidence on which to base a comparison of the degree of isolation of Orange County mothers with that of nineteenth-century mothers. No doubt the circumstances of the two groups are similar, and today's family continues the trend of isolation from neighborhood and kin which was established by the classical nuclear family. The chief difference is that now most mothers work outside the home, making daily contacts that were not available to their nineteenth-century counterparts.

If the exchange of parental affection for bodily gratification on the child's part no longer characterizes the feeding period, that conclusion applies even more clearly to the next developmental phase, toilet training. Mothers in the oedipal family were obsessively concerned with the child's cleanliness. Historians have noted the similarity of this trait with the values of cleanliness, punctuality, and orderliness in industrial society.[20] No doubt these middle-class mothers were also reacting against what they regarded as the unhealthy slovenliness of working-class (and in Europe peasant and aristocratic) children whose parents were casual if not negligent about separating the child from its wastes. Nineteenth-century physicians and writers on child care strongly insisted on early, strict toilet training as a key to the child's moral well-being. The standard sanction against the child's resistance was not corporal punishment but the withdrawal of love.

In Orange County today, judging by the evidence of my sample, things are considerably different. Only half the children are toilet trained by two years of age. Girls are trained earlier than boys, with 60 percent of the girls and only 34 percent of the boys trained by the age of two. I should mention that this is the *only* significant difference in child rearing by sex of child in my study, a difference that is probably due to the more rapid development of girls rather than to any variation in their treatment during this stage.[21] These findings indicate that middle-class children are being trained significantly later than in earlier times. People tend to assume that their own child-rearing practices are "normal" or "natural," but that is far from the case. For example, an eminent American doctor stated as late as 1931, "There is general agreement that training to use a vessel for bowel-movements should

---

[20]Peter Cominos, "Late Victorian Sexual Respectability and the Social System," *International Review of Social History* 8 (1963), 18–48, 216–50.

[21]Chi-square = 5.297 with 1 degree of freedom; p = 0.021. Contingency coefficient = .1395. Lambda = .1154 with sex of child as the dependent variable. Uncertainty coefficient = .0144 with sex of child as the dependent variable.

begin very young, as young as six weeks or two months of age."[22] Such early training was an example of the practice of intruding on the child's bodily functions, with parents insisting that the child control them even before it is physically able to do so. The late training practiced today signifies that parents, abandoning the practice of the oedipal family, permit the child to enjoy its body.

The mothers also abandoned the traditional sanction imposed for failure to comply. Only 2 mothers out of 290 said they told the child they would not love him or her if he or she did not use the potty. This finding may reflect the mothers' attitude about toilet training more than it does their practice. Even so, it represents a drastic shift from the attitude of the oedipal family. A similarly small number of mothers admit that they spank the child to achieve toilet training. Some 10 percent use scolding and getting angry as a sanction, instances that should be added to the number of those who withdraw their love, since these methods imply such a withdrawal. The vast majority respond to a refusal to use the potty by encouraging the child to do better next time.

In addition to new sanctions, the Orange County families deviate from the oedipal family by sharing the task of toilet training with spouse/partners, more than half of whom (57 percent) helped with toilet training often or regularly. This finding is another indication that the rigid role distinctions of the classical nuclear family are disappearing. Middle-class parents today, however, receive little assistance from kin and friends in this child-rearing task. They are probably as isolated from support systems as their earlier counterparts. In sum, data about the toilet-training phase, like that on the feeding phase, indicates that the sampled parents today no longer fit the pattern of the past.

The child's mastery over its body is most sorely tested over the issue of touching the genitals or what is known as childhood masturbation. Such activity was the *bête noir* of the oedipal family, a sign of the most serious moral infamy. Doctors in the nineteenth century warned parents of the dire consequences of masturbation among five year olds: pimples, headaches, deformities, and fatal diseases were the sure result.[23] Even in the 1930s experts encouraged parents to be sure their children were physically exhausted when they went to bed so that the

[22]Helen T. Woolley, "Eating, Sleeping and Elimination," in *Handbook of Child Psychology* (Worcester, Mass.: Clark University Press, 1931), p. 52.
[23]See Mary S. Hartman, "Child-Abuse as Self-Abuse: Two Victorian Cases," *History of Childhood Quarterly* 2 (Fall 1974), 221–48.

problem would be avoided, though by then the hyperbole was gone.[24] Reacting against Christian notions of original sin, the middle classes of the past regarded children as "innocent," and defined innocence as an absence of sexuality. Parents reserved their sternest sanctions for trespasses below the waist.

Today the child's little pleasures are treated differently, or at least such is the claim of the respondents. In the first place the general atmosphere about sexuality in the home is different from that in the oedipal family, with its Victorian reserve on these matters. Two-thirds of the mothers allow their small children to roam the house in the nude, presenting the child with a neutral attitude to his or her nudity. Also, more than 85 percent of the parents allow the child to see them in the nude, an indication to the child that the body is not a forbidden object. Almost all mothers note that their child is aware of sexual difference and is interested in human reproduction. In this environment the child tends to accept the body as a natural fact rather than to develop Victorian fears of the flesh.[25] In Orange County mothers report that they are aware that their child touches its genitals and that they tend to ignore the behavior. Two families punish their child for touching its genitals or warn that someone else will do so. A few parents (5 percent) encourage the activity and a few (2 percent) strongly discourage it. Most (62 percent) do neither.

In the oedipal family the habitual sanction against childhood masturbation for boys was the infamous threat of castration. For girls, there is very little evidence of masturbation, although, since grown women were regarded as asexual, it is likely that masturbation by girls presented such a case of cognitive dissonance that it could not be recognized as such. In the case of boys, castration threats were a matter of course. For example, in the case of "little Hans," Freud reported a conversation between Hans and his mother. When Hans was three and a half "his mother found him with his hand to his penis. She threatened him in these words: 'If you do that, I shall send for Dr. A. to cut off your widdler. And then what'll you widdle with?' "[26]

---

[24]Woolley, "Eating, Sleeping and Elimination," p. 67.

[25]One historian, Peter Gay, has attempted to revise our attitude about Victorian antisexuality. See *The Bourgeois Experience: Victoria to Freud*, vol. 1: *The Education of the Senses* (New York: Oxford University Press, 1984). Yet even he is hard put to prove his case in the matter of childhood masturbation.

[26]Sigmund Freud, "Analysis of a Phobia in a Five-Year Old Boy," trans. in *The Sexual Enlightenment of Children*, ed. Philip Rieff (New York: Macmillan, 1966), p. 49.

Freud reports these words without any indication that they are unusual.

Among those in my sample who discouraged masturbation, none, I am bound to report, uttered such threats. Only two mothers told their child that touching the genitals was dangerous to their health. Fewer said they "angrily" discourage masturbation than said they were "angry" with their child for not using the potty. Many (23 percent) said they "calmly told the child not to do it." Only 2 percent of those who discouraged the activity did so strongly. In the third stage of child development, as in the previous two, the contemporary middle-class family avoids the oedipal strategy of intensifying the child's ambivalent feelings by coercing an exchange of parental love for bodily gratification.

Part of the effectiveness of the oedipal strategy in the nineteenth century derived from the isolation of the child from adults and from children outside the nuclear family. Parents, and perhaps a servant or two, were thought to be the only salutary influences for the child. The urban street was considered a dangerous, dirty place. During the early years the child was sequestered in the apartment or town house as much as possible. With severely restricted contacts, the child's emotional ties to its immediate family were intensified. Such "explosive intimacy" multiplied the effect of the child's ambivalent feelings toward its parents.[27] Perhaps this situation helps to explain why Freud discovered strong love feelings in the child for the parent of the opposite sex.

Although the middle-class Orange County family is likewise isolated from the external world, the child is not sequestered in the home. Mothers report that their children play with other children frequently (77 percent), visit their homes (56 percent), and are sent to pre-schools (81 percent) and day-care centers (34 percent). A significant minority of the children spend considerable periods with relatives. Consequently, these children have more contact with adults outside the family than did their nineteenth-century counterparts, establishing bonds with a variety of adults. More important, from an early age they encounter children outside the family, also finding in them objects for their feelings. In this context their parents remain the most important people in their lives, but there is some reduction in the intensity of intrafamilial relations in comparison with the oedipal family.

[27]Stephen Kern, "Explosive Intimacy: Psychodynamics of the Victorian Family," *History of Childhood Quarterly* 1 (Winter 1974), 437–62.

The comparison of the emotional structure of the oedipal and contemporary families during the early stages of the child's development reveals dramatic changes. Parents have abandoned the oedipal strategy over the course of a century, though the precise pace of the change at any time is difficult to determine. We can, however, compare the situation today with that of thirty years ago, because Robert Sears studied 379 mothers in the Boston area in the mid-1950s asking questions very similar to those in my study.[28] In general, Sears's findings fall midway between the oedipal family and the Orange County family of the mid-1980s. Only 29 percent of Sears's families fed children on demand, and more of the schedule feeders were rigid than in my study. Far more of Sears's families toilet trained their children before two years of age than mine: a full 80 percent completed training by two years. Another great difference in the studies concerns the child's sexuality. Sears's mothers tended not to permit nudity in the home: 60 percent allowed no nudity at all or at most allowed it only on the way to and from the bathroom. Half of Sears's families did not allow their children to touch their genitals and another 25 percent discouraged it. An astonishing 40 percent of his mothers said they never noticed the child masturbating, compared to 7 percent in my study, testimony to the effects of the "sexual revolution" of the 1960s and 1970s.[29] While Sears's findings suggest considerable change from the oedipal family to the 1950s, they also indicate an even more rapid period of transition from the 1950s to the 1980s.

Sociologists have observed for a decade that the classical nuclear family is a waning institution. Based on the criteria of one partner for life and strict sex-role segregation with only the husband working outside the home, the nuclear family comprises less than 10 percent of the whole. For the middle-class family in Orange County, the emo-

[28]These results were published as Robert Sears et al., *Patterns of Child Rearing* (Evanston, Ill.: Row, Peterson, 1957). Working at Harvard University, Sears interviewed mothers in a laboratory setting, whereas my study has been limited to a questionnaire. Sears's sample was significantly different from mine. About half his respondents were from the working class (174). Because, as mentioned, the twentieth-century working-class family resembles the nineteenth-century *middle-class* family in child rearing patterns and because Sears did not report the results for each class separately, his findings are weighted toward the oedipal pattern. Nonetheless his results differ from mine to such an extent that it is unlikely that class accounts for all the variance. Sears's respondents, like mine, were primarily white, but he had more Catholics and Jews than were in my sample, no doubt because of the difference in the location of the studies.

[29]Ibid., pp. 78, 109, 193, 200.

tional heart of the nuclear family—its mechanism of personality formation by intensifying ambivalence in the child, its pattern of exchanging parental love for bodily gratification in the early phases of development—has also disappeared. Instead, today's families allow the child considerable exploration and enjoyment of his or her body. By being flexible with feeding schedules or feeding on demand; by toilet training relatively late in the child's development; by allowing the child to touch its genitals, roam the house in the nude, and see nude adults; by encouraging questions about human reproduction, middle-class Orange County child rearing places positive value on the child's bodily impulses. By exposing the child to adults and children outside the home, parents defuse to some extent the emotional intensity of the child's bonding with them. By giving the child considerable leeway in making its own rules, parents encourage autonomous ego development.

The pattern of age and sex hierarchies in the sample is also considerably at variance with the oedipal family. Parental imposition of authority over children has lessened dramatically. Mothers were asked if they direct the child's play or permit the child to determine what its own activities will be. One-third of the sample reported that they rarely or never direct the child's play. Only 2 percent said they always direct the child's play, as is the tendency in the oedipal family. Parents are also reluctant to impose strict rules on the child: only 24 percent noted that they do so often or always, while 35 percent reported that they do so rarely or never. If one is to judge by what mothers report in the questionnaire—and let me remind the reader at this point that my study tests only attitudes, not behavior—the child is encouraged to take responsibility for itself, to learn the lesson of self-direction not by a forced internalization of parental demands, as was the case in the oedipal family, but by the exploration of its desires and needs. The parenting style in Orange County is far less authoritarian than was the case in the oedipal family.

One may argue the merits of such a relaxation of authoritarian child-rearing styles, an issue of staggering complexity and great controversy. To some extent the optimum degree of structure varies from child to child. Some children thrive on tight adult regulation of their behavior while others furiously resist it. Even so, evidence of childrens' response to authority is not an adequate criterion by which to evaluate this issue. Parents' views must be considered. The influence of other adults (relatives, teachers, and friends of the family) and the media must be added into the equation, both factually (what is their authority) and normatively (what ought to be their authority). As we will see, relaxation of parental authority has been accompanied, among my sample families, by increased "authority" of figures from the child's subculture as they are presented to the child through the media as well as from adults outside the family, such as preschool teachers. It is difficult to judge whether the overall mix of authority on Orange County children is in sum greater or less than that of the oedipal family. Yet the diffusion of authority over the child to a multiplicity of rule-making social agents constitutes a situation in which the child confronts conflicting values, styles, and role models. This situation is very different from that of the child in the oedipal family.

My study indicates that the division of roles between parents is infinitely more flexible today than in the nineteenth century, an indication of the waning of patriarchy, at least in the attitudes reflected in the questionnaire. In 81 percent of the sample parents reported that they share the decision on major purchases; 60 percent share financial decisions; two-thirds share child-rearing decisions; 50 percent share child-rearing tasks. Responses were egalitarian concerning other household chores: 23 percent share housecleaning, and 16 percent share cooking, while spouse/partners do most of the yard work and home repairs. Sharp gender separation appears to be fading in decisions and chores, a vast change from the nineteenth century. Patriarchy, or the general authority of husbands over wives, men over women, however, is not yet dead. Most women work outside the home and yet bear a disproportionate share of the work within the home. Since hired child care is neither plentiful nor cheap, contemporary women pay a heavy price for the degree of emancipation they have won from earlier restrictions. Even so, the rigid gender roles of the oedipal family are discredited and slowly disappearing.

The middle-class Orange County family of the 1980s presents a far more open emotional structure than that of the oedipal family. Children can be heard as well as seen; their desires count for something. The child's body and feelings are validated by parents and given expression outside the home. Parents are no longer legally and morally stereotyped by gender to the same degree as in earlier times. Family members want more from life than the nineteenth-century goals of social respectability and economic success. Organized in the pursuit of these goals, the nineteenth-century families single-mindedly calculated and planned daily life for their attainment. The oedipal family was a shrine of instrumental rationality. By contrast, the Orange County family seeks a wider range of accomplishments. In addition to social and economic success, which demand calculating rationality, today's family pursues emotional and sexual fulfillment. Mothers report that their families engage in a wide range of leisure activities, suggesting a life-style that balances immediate enjoyment with long-term security. The vaunted ability of the oedipal family to accumulate wealth by savings is a forgotten ideal. In the contemporary family context the child is no doubt both bewildered and enthralled by what life has to offer.

Given these new trends in child rearing, children will likely grow up with a greater sense of the need for sensual gratification and will give a greater value as adults to their emotional fulfillment. They will be less driven by superego demands, less prone to defer gratification for success, and they will have less rigid egos, since they are not burdened by the need for systematically repressing bodily impulses. Since they live in dual-career families or families with working single parents and since their parents tend to divide household work between themselves, the child's role models and images of adults (or ego ideals) will be less gender-based than those of oedipal children. It is possible as well that as adults the Orange County children will bring to politics new demands based less on the work ethic of the past than on a more rounded vision of a fulfilling life.

There are, however, other aspects of life in which the Orange County family continues to promote the oedipal family pattern. Today's family remains an isolated unit with a clear sense of the privacy of domestic interactions. Perhaps even more than the oedipal family, the contemporary family is remote from relatives and, as a unit, is not actively involved in the daily life of the surrounding community. My sample was taken from cities that are essentially bedroom communities, very different from the urban setting of the nineteenth-century middle class. Isolated from networks of sociability, the middle-class Orange County family is open to the influence of the wider society, especially to consumer culture, and it has even fewer resources than the oedipal family to resist outside incursions. New technologies, such as the television, the video cassette recorder, and the computer, bring that outer world into family life with awesome realism and power. These technologies, though in principle they might be the occasion for family gatherings and discussions, actually work to divide family members from one another, to encourage isolated activities within the home, and to deflect the attention of family members away from one another toward individual subcultures.[30] Cartoons and MTV for children, soap operas for women, and sports for men, to use the case of television, constitute miniworlds within the home which are neither like communities in the traditional sense of face-to-face interactions nor like single-person activities such as novel reading, which was so popular in the nineteenth century. In these respects the new family pattern promotes a deterioration of public life, at least in the traditional sense.[31]

To pursue this question further, the findings about child rearing during the first three stages are be correlated with data about parenting style, relations between adults in the family, the family's use of new technologies and its general social characteristics.

Comparisons between child-rearing variables and general family traits, to begin with the last index, yield surprisingly little variance. Since almost all the families are white, racial difference is eliminated. There is also no significant difference in child-rearing methods when cross-tabulated with family income, except that the wealthier families, as one might expect, hire more help for child rearing than do the less wealthy. This finding is explained in part by the fact that the wealthier families are also the older families. The younger families have lower incomes simply because they are at earlier stages of their careers than the older families. In all likelihood the sample is highly homogeneous in social class. Differences within the sample, one may deduce, are due to life-style choices, not income.

Nor do religious differences account for much of the variation in child-rearing methods. Jews and Protestants are somewhat more flexible in scheduling the feeding of the child than Mormons and Catholics. Jews wean their children later than Catholics and Protestants. Catholics begin toilet training earlier than the rest, especially those with no religious preference. Spouse/partners of Jews and Protestants help with toilet training more than others. Mormons and Catholics are most likely to discourage nudity among their children and to forbid

---

[30]For the isolating effect of the computer, see the following informative studies: Alladi Venkatesh, "A Conceptualization of the Household/Technology Interaction," in E. C. Hirschman and M. Holbrook, eds., *Advances in Consumer Research* 12 (1985), 189–95; and Nicholas Vitalari, Alladi Venkatesh, and Kjell Gronhaug, "Computing in the Home: Shifts in the Time Allocation Patterns of Households," *Communications of the ACM* 28 (May 1985), 512–22.

[31]Richard Sennett, *The Fall of Public Man* (New York: Knopf, 1977).

their children to see adult family members nude. Mormons especially discourage the child from touching its genitals.[32] These differences do begin to divide the sample into those who are closer to the oedipal family (Mormons and Catholics) from those who are most divergent from it (Jews and nonreligionists), with Protestants falling somewhere in between. While these are interesting and perhaps anticipated results, the variance in child-rearing method due to religious preference does not account for much of the overall variance.

I divided the sample by traditional and nontraditional marital status, the former being those married for the first time (188) and the latter being those never married (8) and those divorced at least once even if currently remarried (94). Since in the oedipal family divorce was rare and unmarried mothers unheard of, the marital status distinction provides another criterion against which to array the families by degree of deviation from that norm. Again, this criterion yielded few significant results. There were a few differences in child-rearing method but no consistent pattern. Mothers married for the first time are not closer to the oedipal paradigm than the rest of the sample. I then divided the sample by mother's occupation, comparing housewives (70) to mothers with careers (220). Once again the results showed little variation: housewives were not closer to the oedipal mother than career women, even though they are similar to nineteenth-century middle-class mothers in their daily occupations. The only difference between housewives and career mothers is that the former rate higher on the narcissism scale: they are more worried than career women about the child's breaking things and are less aware that two-year-olds are defining their own boundaries. It may be that people restricted to domesticity are more likely to manifest these traits. Yet overall the differences are not great.[33]

[32]The frequencies for religious affiliation are as follows: (1) flexible feeding schedule: Jews 74 percent, Protestants 73 percent, Mormons 58 percent, Catholics 60 percent; (2) weaning 1 year or later: Jews 48 percent, Catholics 27 percent, Protestants 24 percent; (3) begin toilet training earlier than 2 years: Catholics 58 percent, next closest are Jews with 48 percent, nonreligionists 38 percent; (4) spouse/partner help with toilet training: Jews 76 percent, Protestants 61 percent, Catholics 46 percent, nonreligionists 53 percent; (5) discourage child's nudity: Mormons 86 percent, Catholics 22 percent, Jews 12 percent, Protestants 8 percent; (6) discourage child from touching its genitals: Mormons 100 percent, Jews 35 percent, Catholics 32 percent, Protestants 31 percent.

[33]On fear of the child's breaking things: housewives 12 percent, career mothers 6 percent. On thinking that two-year-olds are defining their own boundaries: housewives 60 percent, career mothers 70 percent. On all other child-rearing variables, the frequencies dividing housewives from career mothers were less than 5 percent.

From these analyses I reach the important conclusion that differ-ences in the emotional structure of the family within a white middle-class sample are the consequence of parenting styles, not income, religion, marital status, or mother's occupation. No doubt some vari-able not tested in this study may correlate with differences in parent-ing style. But it seems to me that my finding suggests that family relationships have become the object of intentional social practices, that partners define their family type as part of their deliberate choice of life-style very much like Foucault's classical Greeks. In other words, once the classical nuclear family has been rejected by the white middle class, which, as I have shown, is the case for the families I studied in contemporary Orange County, the major social determinants may no longer adequately account for family structure. Since the oedipal fam-ily is gone and family patterns are in flux, partners have a degree of freedom in choosing a type of authority and love relation with their children. The question remains: what are those types and how great is the variety among them?

To answer this question I created models of three family types. To distinguish the family types I use "political" terms, but these are not meant to reflect actual political allegiances, which often do not corre-late directly with family type. Instead, the terms designate only the degree of difference of the family from the oedipal family. The "con-servative family" is that in which parents still exert considerable au-thority over their child's daily life and in which adult roles conform to some extent to the gender divisions of the nineteenth century. The "democratic family" is that in which parents grant a degree of auton-omy to their children and serious effort is made to share family deci-sions and tasks between adults. The "experimental family" is that in which the child is encouraged to define some of its own rules and in which adults attempt to divide decisions and tasks *equally*. I then selected those variables that were good indicators of the extent of the difference between the oedipal and the Orange County family, as well as those values for each variable that best fit each family type (see Table 6). While the relationship between the values and the family types is somewhat arbitrary, I consistently used the criterion of degree of difference from the oedipal family pattern as a guide. The frequency of family types are 19 percent conservative, 36 percent democratic, and 45 percent experimental, an interesting result. Some 80 percent of the sample are families in which participants report that the hierarchies of age and sex, as well as the pattern of authority and love during the

Table 6. Variables and values by family type

	Value		
Variable	Conservative	Democratic	Experimental
Feeding	on schedule	both	on demand
Spouse's help	rarely	sometimes	half or more
Toilet training		younger than 2	older than 2
Spouse's help	once or never	often	regularly
See nude adults	rarely/never	sometimes	often/always
Ignore masturbation	rarely/never	sometimes	often/always
Rearing decisions	mother	mostly mother	adults & child
Who does cooking	mother	mostly mother	adults equally
Who does cleaning	mother	mostly mother	adults equally
Impose strict rules	always/often	sometimes	rarely/never
Who makes rules	always mother	mostly mother	adults & child

child's early years, varies considerably from those of the oedipal family.

There are also clear differences among the Orange County families according to their degree of difference from the oedipal family. Like the oedipal family, the "conservative" families feed their children more on a schedule and the spouse/partners help with feeding less than in the "democratic" and "experimental" families. But during toilet training and sexuality stages of the child the "conservative" families were not closer than the other types to the oedipal family. Regarding the tasks of cooking and cleaning the house and the decisions about how to raise the child, the "experimental" family was farthest from nineteenth-century gender roles, the "democratic" family was next farthest; and the "conservative" family was closest.

A confirmation of the family types is disclosed when they are cross-tabulated against both the variables for adult direction of childrens' play and for the age at which children are permitted to set their own rules (see Tables 7 and 8). Mothers read the following paragraph: "There are many activities in a child's life which parents may regulate or allow the child to regulate himself or herself. Parents differ greatly in the way they impose limits on these activities. Examples of activities which may or may not be strictly regulated are the child's bedtime, the child's choice of friends, the number of hours a day the child watches television. The following questions ask about the manner and the extent to which you regulate these and similar activities of your child." Mothers were then asked if they or their spouse/partner and other

Table 7. Directing play

Do you, your spouse/partner, and other adults in your family direct the child's play or permit the child to decide on its own activities?

	Always	Sometimes	Never
Conservative	23%	54%	23%
Democratic	15%	52%	33%
Experimental	10%	46%	44%

Table 8. Allowing the child to set rules

If you allow your child to set its own rules for his or her activities, at what age do you do so?

	Over 8 yrs.	6 to 8 yrs.	Under 6
Conservative	70%	17%	13%
Democratic	25%	22%	53%
Experimental	8%	5%	87%

adults in their family direct the child's play or permit the child to decide on its own activities (see Table 7). Conservative families reported most often that they always direct the child's play and least often that they rarely direct the child's play. Experimental families reported least often that they always direct the child play and most often that they rarely do so. Parents were also asked at what age they permitted their child to set its own rules (see Table 8). The table reveals that the conservative families permitted rule setting latest and experimental families permitted it earliest. On both questions there were serious differences between the family types, differences that form line of increasing divergence from the oedipal family pattern. These findings indicate that the statistical construction of the three family types is valid and that Orange County families, while rejecting the oedipal model, may be arrayed by their degree of difference from that model.

More plainly put, among middle-class white Orange County families with at least one child six or younger there is serious disagreement about what the age and sex hierarchies should be like. In the conservative group, the smallest of the three in my sample (19 percent), adults to some extent maintain the traditional gender-role divisions and sustain a relatively high degree of adult authority over children. In the experimental group, the largest in my sample (45 percent), adults report that they have completely abandoned gender-defined roles, equally sharing tasks and decisions, and that they have considerably abandoned parental domination of children, refusing to impose strict rules on them. In the democratic group, constituting (36 percent) of the sample, family arrangements fall in between the other groups.

If Lasch's thesis about narcissistic families were correct, the experimental family would show the highest correlation with variables for narcissism and the conservative family the lowest since the experimental families appear to be the least involved with their children and the conservative families the most involved. Exactly the opposite is the case: the conservative families rated highest on the narcissism questions and the experimental families the lowest. This result indicates that "egalitarian" relations between adults and children are not a sign of indifference on the adults' part, as Lasch would have us believe. On the contrary, the experimental parents are as concerned as the other types about their children, but they are more aware of the border between their own egos and those of their children than are the parents in the other families. The results suggest that Lasch and others who bemoan contemporary family trends make a hasty and faulty equivalence between authoritarian, patriarchal families with gender-differentiated roles, on the one hand, and the child's maximal development as an independent, capable adult, on the other hand.

If the families of the 1980s disagree about the pattern of age and sex hierarchies, they are fundamentally uncertain about how to structure parental authority and love during the early stages of child development. The findings of the study support no clear pattern in this regard in relation to the conservative, democratic, and experimental family types. Perhaps the questionnaire itself was not drawn in such a way that it could elicit a detailed picture of such subtle issues. Or it might be that rapid social changes, along with the new pattern of age and sex hierarchies revealed here, has not yet resulted in definable emotional structures.

There is a third possibility, one that constitutes the conclusion of this book. It may be that a coherent structure of authority and love, such as the oedipal pattern of trading bodily gratification for parental love, is characteristic of families that are emotionally isolated from the wider society. The middle-class Orange County family of the 1980s is decidedly not so isolated. In my sample children are in preschools and most mothers work outside the home. Both adults and children experience significant relationships outside the home. The family, then, is a *segmented* group, dividing its time between family and nonfamily relations, suggesting that Orange County as a whole is a "segmented metropolis." As a segmented group, in which each individual in part follows a life course separate from the others, it follows that the love-authority structure in the family may no longer constitute a crucial determinant of the child's experience and personality development.

The segmentation of family life goes beyond the question of individuated activities outside the home. The penetration of the home by electronically mediated communication systems, or the mode of information, ensures continuous contact for each family member with its particular subculture. Through the use of television, telephones, Walkmen, and video cassette recorders, the child, while physically in the home, receives communications from people outside the family. The widespread use of televisions, VCRs, and computers by Orange County families, as demonstrated by the high proportion of families who own these devices and use them frequently, mitigates the intensity of family interactions,[34] permitting a diffusion of emotional bonding. In the questionnaire, mothers disclosed that leisure activities, even watching television, only sporadically involved the family as a whole. Visiting amusement parks or public parks, camping, going to the movies, visiting relatives or friends, going shopping—all these activities, which could done as a family unit, were only rarely the occasion of family solidarity. The activity most often done by the family as a unit was dining in restaurants, an indication of the wealth of the families sampled but also a sign of the complexity of their lives, since restaurants relieve the pressure of preparing meals.

Middle-class families in Orange County are at a crossroads. Surrounded by an emerging new social formation, the mode of information, families have rejected the classical nuclear-family pattern. They are testing new family structures, some of which reject to a considerable degree earlier forms of domination in the family. One senses a tremendous burden on these micro-units of society and, accordingly, a deep contradiction in the emerging social formation. These Orange County families have great ambitions: they want to remove restric-

---

[34]Few of the respondents, however, admitted that they or anyone in their family watched television more than three or four hours a week, considerably below the national average. It must be concluded that their responses on this question were less than accurate, itself an interesting indication of ambivalence about new communications media.

tions on women's life choices; they want to achieve emotional and sexual gratification; they want to develop in their children an ability for self-directed personal growth; they want to enjoy the sophisticated technologies available to them. These goals suggest a type of integration between the family and the community unique to the mode of information, one that places new demands on the social formation: families now want high-quality, plentiful day care, even in workplaces; richer community life; extensive sharing of information; and activities made possible by new technologies. Yet the social formation resists the changes implied in these demands. The modern family thus constitutes itself as a segmented unit, adapting its goals to a recalcitrant environment and bearing what must be the great stress of experimentation without adequate support.

Index

Library of Congress Cataloging-in-Publication Data

Poster, Mark.
    Critical theory and poststructuralism.

    Includes index.
       1. Foucault, Michel. 2. Critical theory.
3. Structuralism. I. Title.
B2430.F724P67 1989   142   89–7262
ISBN 0–8014–2336–8 (alk. paper)
ISBN 0–8014–9588–1 (pbk. : alk. paper)